UTOPIANISM AND MARXISM

UTOPIANISM
AND
MARXISM

VINCENT GEOGHEGAN

METHUEN
London and New York

First published in 1987 by
Methuen & Co. Ltd
11 New Fetter Lane, London EC4P 4EE

Published in the USA by
Methuen & Co.
in association with Methuen, Inc.
29 West 35th Street, New York NY 10001

© 1987 Vincent Geoghegan

Printed in Great Britain by Richard Clay (The Chaucer Press) Ltd,
Bungay, Suffolk

British Library Cataloguing in Publication Data

Geoghegan, Vincent
  Utopianism and Marxism.
  1. Utopian socialism
  I. Title
  321'.07   HX632
  ISBN 0–416–08062–6
  ISBN 0–416–08072–3 Pbk

Library of Congress Cataloging in Publication Data

Geoghegan, Vincent.
  Utopianism and Marxism.
  Bibliography: p.
  Includes index.
  1. Utopias. 2. Socialism. 3. Communism.
I. Title.
HX806.G46 1987 335'.02 87–12333
ISBN 0–416–08062–6
ISBN 0–416–08072–3 (pbk.)

CONTENTS

ACKNOWLEDGEMENTS

I would like to thank the following for their great help in reading various drafts of this work: Bob Eccleshall, Mick Cox, Richard Jay, John LeJuen and Bernard Crick. Richard Kuper made some useful early suggestions. I received valuable feedback from papers I presented at two conferences organized by The Society for Utopian Studies in St Louis (1984 – convened by Lyman Sargent) and Monterey (1986 – convened by Samson Knoll), also from a paper presented at The Political Thought Conference, Oxford (1984 – convened by Bill Stafford). Nancy Marten of Methuen has been both encouraging and most helpful in getting this work finally to press. A slightly different version of chapter 6 appeared in *Radical Philosophy*, 45 (Spring 1987), entitled 'The realism of utopia' (with thanks to Mike Shortland). A modified version of part of chapter 4 will shortly appear in *San José Studies* (1987), entitled 'The golden age and its return in Marxism' (with thanks to Fauneil J. Rinn). The author and the publishers wish to thank John Berger and Anna Bostock for permission to reproduce their translation of the Mayakovsky poem *The 150,000,000*.

INTRODUCTION: IN PRAISE OF UTOPIANISM

I wish to defend that 'unrealistic', 'irrational', 'naive', 'self-indulgent', 'unscientific', 'escapist', 'élitist', activity known as utopianism. The predominant technical usage of the term 'utopian'[1] has been as a definition of the shining cities, just polities and hedonistic paradises lovingly described by such authors as Campanella, Bacon and Bellamy. Two great works of Renaissance political thought can set the scene. Thomas More's *Utopia* (1516), with its pun 'utopia' ('no-place') 'eutopia' ('good-place'), created the word for, and most celebrated example of, an alternative society. Utopia, the narrator says, is

> not only the best country in the world, but the only one that has any right to call itself a republic . . . The Utopian way of life provides . . . the happiest basis for a civilized community . . . They've eliminated the root-causes of ambition, political conflict, and everything like that.[2]

A few years earlier, Machiavelli, in *The Prince* (1513), had championed the cause of 'realism' against such creations:

> since my intention is to say something that will prove of practical use to the inquirer, I have thought it proper to represent things as they are in real truth, rather than as they are imagined. Many have dreamed up republics and principalities which have never in truth been known to exist.[3]

On what grounds, therefore, can the production and consumption of these ideal worlds be justified?

The classic utopia anticipates and criticizes. Its alternative

1

fundamentally interrogates the present, piercing through existing societies' defensive mechanisms – common sense, realism, positivism and scientism. Its unabashed and flagrant otherness gives it a power which is lacking in other analytical devices. By playing fast and loose with time and space, logic and morality, and by thinking the unthinkable, a utopia asks the most awkward, the most embarrassing questions. As an imaginative construction of a whole society, the utopia can bring into play the rich critical apparatus of the literary form and a sensitivity to the holistic nature of society, enabling it to mock, satirize, reduce the prominent parts, to illuminate and emphasize the neglected, shadowy, hidden parts – and to show the inter-relatedness – of the existing system.

Utopia can be seen as the good alternative, the outline of a better future, an 'ought' to the current 'is'. The possibility of such a future helps undermine the complacency and overcome the inertia of existing society by showing that it is neither eternal nor archetypal but merely one form amongst many. This need not lead to teleology (i.e. 'this is your future'), for the alternative has many shapes. A past utopia, for example, may be considered impossible or undesirable but none the less be thought to contain gold-bearing seams; or a utopia might be devised as a type of mental game playing with possibilities and exploring hypotheses; or it might be used to speculate about the fate or destiny of specific social groups. Popperians, who speak of the unverifiable nature of utopianism, would do well to consider the predictive power of past utopians, as society caught up with their ideals. The new has often taken its first faltering steps in this medium.

There is more to utopianism, however, than the classic utopia. Following Bloch and Mannheim,[4] we can speak of a utopian disposition, a utopian impulse or mentality, of which the classic utopia is but one manifestation. This impulse is grounded in the human capacity, and need, for fantasy; the perpetual conscious and unconscious rearranging of reality and one's place in it. It is the attempt to create an environment in which one is truly at ease. Freud's position, 'We may lay it down that a happy person never phantasises, only an unsatisfied one',[5] must be rejected in this stark form. J. L. Singer is surely correct in arguing, on the basis of modern research, that 'to be human is also to be subject to daydreaming'.[6] We can, perhaps, reconcile these two stances by examining Freud's explanation for his remarkable assertion. 'The motive forces of phantasies', he argues, 'are unsatisfied wishes, and every single phantasy is the fulfilment of a wish, a correction of unsatisfying reality'.[7] Clearly, the more unsatisfying reality is and the more marginal and disadvantaged one is, the more likely it is that one will dream of better times. Singer's own work amongst subcultural groups in the USA supports this hypothesis.[8] In this sense fantasy can readily lend itself to the struggles of out-groups in society. But really no-one can be 'happy' in Freud's sense of the word, for no matter how well integrated one is in society there remain unfulfilled wishes and desires. Freud in fact virtually acknowledges this: 'I believe that most people construct phantasies at times in their lives'.[9] In short, fantasy would seem to be a constant in any conceivable society.

This impulse can be found at all levels of activity: in leisurely dreaming, in the various forms of personal display, in eroticism and art, as well as in the more familiar form of futuristic blueprints. It can of course take the form of mere escape from a hostile world. James Thurber's 'The Secret Life of Walter Mitty'[10] and Keith Waterhouse's Billy Liar ('Lying in bed, I abandoned the facts again and was back in Ambrosia!')[11] are excellent evocations of this phenomenon. But it also can, and does, issue forth directly and indirectly in political form. Radical ideologies display this most obviously. An image of a fit life for the individual is at the centre of early liberal attacks on absolutism: the Leveller vision of a community of independent citizens in which basic civil rights were enshrined. Early socialism, as we shall see, was self-consciously anticipatory. Nationalists from the eighteenth century onwards have, usually in imperial contexts, created the vision of their distinct nation which has served as a goal for political action. They have, to use Benedict Anderson's phrase, created 'imagined communities'[12] out of the materials of historical experience, language, geography and so forth. Women too, in the struggle against their oppression, have operated with conceptions of what female liberation will look like in practice.

Again, utopianism is also present in the so-called 'limited' or 'realist' ideologies. Thatcherite conservatism is a glaring example of right-wing utopianism, with its summoning up of the supposed glories of Victorian Britain as a model and its underlying, far-fetched beliefs that, for example, the market is essentially a benign institution and that brutalizing youngsters with short, sharp shocks somehow improves them.[13] However, even the conservatism of those who consider Thatcherism to be dangerous radicalism – who speak of conservatism as 'moderate', 'non-ideological', 'dispositional', 'commonsensical', etc. – is utopian. The collection of essays edited by Hobsbawm and Ranger, evocatively entitled *The Invention of Tradition*,[14] reveals the degree of normative artifice involved in the so-called 'traditional'. The patrician conservatives may not elevate a mythical nineteenth-century *laissez-faire* Britain, but their idealization of a happy, ranked society of once upon a time is equally normative, equally utopian. Even the most complacent of conservatives selectively considers the present in the imagination and invests it with the sceptre of the ideal – the litany of monarchy, property, custom, having the same nature as a radical's republic, common ownership, reason. Such conservatives utopianize the present.

The utopian impulse is therefore not necessarily politically progressive, as some of its supporters wish to claim; it can clearly issue forth in malignant forms. National Socialism is perhaps the clearest example of this with its appalling vision of a thousand-year Aryan *reich*, a vision at the very heart of contemporary neo-fascism. Liberals are quite right in seeing Auschwitz as a poisonous fruit of utopianism. They spoil their case by arguing that Auschwitz is the inevitable consequence of utopianism.

This latter view was also fuelled by the historical experience of Stalinism. The gap between rhetoric and reality in the Soviet Union was seen variously as evidence of the obtuseness, fanaticism or self-interestedness of utopians. The accompanying dystopian literature from Zamyatin to Orwell, with its portrayal of intolerant, élitist, uniform and stagnant societies, was in turn harnessed to this attack on utopianism itself. The idea that the way out of a dystopia lies not in the rejection of utopianism but in its refinement was not entertained. Rejecting the west's pious nostrums of Democracy, Capitalism and Christ, a number of east-European socialists came to develop utopian critiques of their respective societies. As we shall see, Rudolf Bahro's significantly-entitled *Die Alternative* was one such attempt.

Turning to more indirect forms of the utopian impulse, we might note its presence in architecture and in town and country planning. The city orientation of past utopians has often been noticed. Writers such as Campanella, in his *The City of the Sun*, dwell lovingly on the shape, size and position of the buildings and thoroughfares of their urban paradises. Visionary architects have in turn sought through their designs to build the perfect environment for humanity; a case in point being the work of the eighteenth-century French architect, Boulée, whose designs included the awesome – and unbuilt – Newton Cenotaph. Sometimes, as in the case of Albert Speer's Nazi monumentalism, this has been at the service of malign vision or, as decaying tower blocks reveal, based upon inadequate conceptions. None the less, there is clearly a modern role for self-consciously visionary planning and architecture, either directly as part of a general democratic planning/political process, or indirectly – as Robert Fishman reveals in his discussion of Filarete, Ledoux and Le Corbusier – through the provision of brilliant, if unrealizable, models which can act as a stimulant on the planning/political process.[15]

Another form is to be found in fashion. The current connotation of the word indicates the extent to which taste is manipulated in modern capitalism through the exploitation of dream and fantasy. This process is, however, complex and non-totalitarian. Bodily display can both take issue with the present and suggest another reality. This can happen in a distorted, tragic manner, as with Dickens' Miss Havisham – jilted on her wedding morning she grows old in her wedding clothes: 'I saw', says Pip, 'that the bride within the bridal dress had withered like the dress, and like the flowers, and had no brightness left but the brightness of her sunken eyes'.[16] Her clothes protest against the shattering of, but also embody, her great expectations. Again, in Eugene O'Neill's *Long Day's Journey into Night*, a wedding dress represents the claims, and loss, of happiness to a lonely married woman:

> Oh, how I loved that gown! It was so beautiful! Where is it now, I wonder? I used to take it out from time to time when I was lonely, but it always made me cry . . . I wonder where I hid it? Probably in one of the old trunks in the attic. Some day I'll have to look.[17]

More positively, the general capacity for, and delight in, texture, shape and colour could issue forth expressively in a genuine cultural transformation. Elizabeth Wilson's evocatively-entitled *Adorned in Dreams* sensitively analyses the double-edged nature of fashion, yet is strongly committed to its utopian dimension:

> Fashion acts as a vehicle for fantasy . . . There will . . . never
> be a human world without fantasy . . . All art draws on
> unconscious fantasy; the performance that is fashion is one
> road from the inner to the outer world . . . [W]e should use
> dress to express and explore our more daring aspirations,
> while respecting those who use it to disguise personal
> inadequacies, real or imagined, or to make themselves feel
> confident or important.[18]

The whole phenomenon of advanced consumerist civilization
cannot be simply dismissed as the product of false consciousness.
Products do manipulate and indoctrinate, as Marcuse argues,
but they also respond to, reflect and stimulate genuine human
needs. Hans Magnus Enzenberger spells out the utopian nature
of this process.

> Goods and shop windows, traffic and advertisements, stores
> and the world of communications, news and packaging,
> architecture and media production, come together to form a
> totality, a permanent theatre, which dominates not only the
> public city centres but also private interiors . . . Yet trickery
> on such a scale is only conceivable if it is based on mass need.
> This need – it is an utopian one – is there. It is in the desire for
> a new ecology, for a breaking down of environmental
> barriers, for an aesthetic which is not limited to the sphere of
> 'the artistic'. These desires are not – or not primarily –
> internalized rules of the game as played by the capitalist
> system. They have physiological roots and can no longer be
> suppressed. Consumption as spectacle is – in parody form –
> the anticipation of an utopian situation.[19]

Given the utopian impulse in its many forms, the classical
practicality critique of utopianism no longer holds water. An
impractical, unrealistic utopianism cannot be counterposed to a
practical, non-utopian realism, for utopianism can issue forth in
both practical and impractical forms. Also, given varying
definitions of reality, the realism/utopianism distinction was
always a difficult one to maintain and easily lent itself to
ideological usage. Thus the vote for women was utopian, the
welfare state was utopian, X, Y, and Z were utopian – but for
whom? As Karl Mannheim noted, 'the representatives of a
given order will label as utopian all conceptions of existence
which *from their point of view* can in principle never be realised'.[20]
Thus Popper's attempt to distinguish 'admissible plans for social

reform' (good) from 'utopianism' (bad), [21] like Oakeshott's similar distinction between the admirable 'pursuit of intimations' and unacceptable 'rationalism'[22] is really a conflict between dreams masquerading as an attack on dreaming.

What then should be the place of utopianism in Marxism? In what follows, I want to argue for a self-consciously utopian Marxism, while examining the role of utopianism in Marx, Engels, and a variety of later Marxists. Firstly, however, let us look at the beginnings of socialism, the period of the utopian socialists, the period out of which Marx and Engels emerged.

CHAPTER 1

THE UTOPIAN SOCIALISTS

The utopian socialists saw themselves as social scientists. 'Utopian' was, for them, a pejorative term, like 'dreamer' or 'visionary', used to describe fanciful schemes divorced from reality. Time and again in their work they asserted their hard-headed, scientific, realistic and practical approach to society. There was nothing 'utopian', as they understood the term, in their methodology. The description of their work as 'utopian' is therefore a retrospective judgement and not a self-definition. The three thinkers discussed in this chapter, Saint-Simon, Owen and Fourier, are clearly utopian in the sense understood in my introduction, in that they all developed visions of an alternative society. Their work is therefore worth examining, not just because of its intrinsic merit (which is great) or because of its later important influence, but also because it raises questions about the way 'utopianism' came to be seen in the later socialist movement.

HENRI SAINT-SIMON 1760–1825

The tag 'utopian socialism' often affixed to the work of Saint-Simon[1] is in danger of concealing more than it reveals. Taking the 'utopian' aspect first: the implicit contrast conventionally suggested in this usage, between unscientific, woolly utopianism on the one hand and solid science on the other, is singularly inapplicable to Saint-Simon. His constant and overarching aim was to construct a *science* of humanity and he drew widely from the learned literature of his day. He is rightly considered to be one of the founders of modern sociology. Whether Saint-Simon was a socialist is a moot point. One can find in his writings statements which are royalist, élitist, racist, authoritarian, thoroughly anti-democratic and which defend property rights and sing the praises of capitalism. What we have here is a thinker witnessing the birth of the modern ideological world, where the battle lines are not yet drawn up and all is still fluid. Neither fish nor fowl, he does not fit into the comforting categories of contemporary debate.

Saint-Simon took great pains to show that his vision of future society was not spun out of mere whimsy but was firmly grounded in existing social tendencies. Human history was not composed of random, disconnected events; rather it was structured and coherent and its internal dynamic and general direction were accessible to scientific analysis. Class is the central category in his theory of history.

The great drama of the modern era consisted of the emergence, within medieval society, of a new class, the industrial, destructive of its host and spearhead of the new golden age. In France (for the details of this process varied from country to country), the starting point was the invasion and settlement of the Franks in the sixth century A.D. The Frankish military leaders were the dominant economic force in society, as they owned most of the land, animals and indeed the indigenous Gaulish peasants and artisans. As a result of the crusades, these Frankish grandees required revenue beyond their means and were forced to sell land to those Gauls who had managed to acquire surpluses. The crusades also stimulated domestic and foreign trade and manufacturing through the creation of new needs: for luxury goods (under the influence of Asiatic tastes) and fine armaments. A further concession of the nobles lay in the freeing of the communes, which gave a fillip to self-government and independence. Thus by the fifteenth century there was a separate class of farmers, artisans and merchants. From this century the French monarchy, in its struggle with the old feudal nobility, forged an alliance with the increasingly powerful industrial sector such that eventually the nobles were fundamentally weakened and, with growing royal dependence on banking and credit, the industrials became *the* most important class in society. Government, however, still remained in the hands of regressive class forces.

A concomitant struggle of ideas was occurring in this period. The feudal Frankish lords were, in their sphere, an improvement on the Roman system they had superseded. Saint-Simon did not subscribe to Renaissance and Enlightenment attempts to exalt the ancient world at the expense of the medieval – for his was a dynamic, linear and essentially perfectionist theory of history. In turn, these nobles had to give way to the more progressive methods of the industrial class. The clergy, in the same way, were the scientific leaders of the medieval world – their conceptions outstripped those of the late Roman empire. From the eleventh century, however, with the introduction of Arab science to Europe, a more sophisticated scientific analysis came to challenge the clerical standpoint, a challenge deepened by British and French science and philosophy since the sixteenth century. Just as feudal and theological interests had been linked in an organic whole, so it was now necessary for the industrial-scientific bloc to usher in a society fully expressing the principles of its existence.

Two points need to be made here. Firstly, productive labour rather than ownership is at the heart of Saint-Simon's class perspective. History is the rise, fall and replacement of successive productive classes. Consequently, Saint-Simon lumps together in the most recent progressive class all productive workers from the proletarian machinist through to the bourgeois factory owner and excludes only idlers such as the nobility, the clergy and their apologists. Thus, writing in 1821, he computed that in France there were 29,500,000 producers and only 500,000 non-producers. He posits an essential unity of interests within this great conglomeration and does not countenance any fundamental conflict between proletariat and bourgeoisie. Secondly, Saint-Simon sees the 'cunning of reason' (to use a Hegelian concept Saint-Simon was unaware of) at work in history. History, in other words, has been made by people unaware of the true nature of their activities. The historical point has, however, been reached where comprehension of the whole process is available to the best scientific brains (of which Saint-Simon is, of course, the most notable!). The task for these gifted individuals is not one of single-handedly engineering the new industrial society out of thin air, for existing social tendencies will inevitably generate this new order, but rather one of making the productive classes fully conscious of their historical duty, thereby effecting a smooth and timely transition.

Since the new society is merely the culmination of current trends, its anticipation will not be abstract and speculative but

concrete and specific. The tragedy of the French Revolution was
that, instead of the industrial class consciously and firmly taking
the lead, the movement fell into the hands of 'jurists and
metaphysicians' who were in thrall to abstract 'rights of man'
[sic] conceptions. These doctrines, once useful in the demolition
of the old order of ideas, did not reflect the scientific direction of
humanity and were always inextricably linked with that old
order. Thus 'the sovereignty of the people' presupposed
'sovereignty by the Grace of God'. Both were products of the
society to be surpassed. 'These two opposing dogmas . . . have
nothing but a reciprocal existence . . . An abstraction . . . gave
rise to an abstraction . . . But now the battle is over'.[2] The high
priest of natural rights, Tom Paine, was himself aware of this
problem when he criticized the French revolutionaries' establishment of a 'universal right of conscience': 'Toleration is not the
opposite of Intolerance, but is the counterfeit of it. Both are
despotisms. The one assumes to itself the right of withholding
Liberty of Conscience, and the other of granting it'.[3] Saint-
Simon was at one, in this respect, with the counter-revolutionary
thinkers of Restoration France, de Maistre and de Bonald (the
latter received a number of favourable mentions in Saint-
Simon's work) and with Edmund Burke. They shared his stress,
though from a very different, imperfectionist perspective, on
the social totality and its complex emergence in history, and the
consequent superficiality and negativeness of the natural rights
radicals. Saint-Simon also polemicized against moralistic
utopianism. There was no point in worrying about the best of all
possible worlds – a meaningless exercise, since the present
necessarily structured all possibility:

> It is no longer a problem of discussing endlessly how to know
> which is the best of governments. There is nothing good,
> there is nothing bad, absolutely speaking. Everything is
> relative – that is the only absolute. Everything is relative
> above all to the times, insofar as social institutions are
> concerned.[4]

The appropriate form of the new society reflects the changes
that have occurred historically in the social function of power. In
feudal times, when the bulk of the population were morally and
intellectually unsophisticated, the more sophisticated minority
had monopolistically to employ punitive force to keep society
functioning. However, the new industrial class merely used

power in their scientific appropriation of nature and, defensively, against the feudal class; their social relationships were based upon the very different principles of peaceful competition and co-operation. This increase and spread of sophistication meant that the old feudal power relationship now acted as a barrier to further development. The productive class would therefore be naturally sympathetic to a scheme of restructuring based upon the elimination of power from all social relationships and its relegation to relationships with nature. In short, they would be attracted to a system which replaced government with administration.

Such a system is not a piece of abstract speculation: it is rather the necessary and logical extension of all previous development. It is not that the producers will somehow become 'converted' to the idea of removing social power: it is that their very existence is already based upon these principles. Saint-Simon cites the cases of the modern credit and banking system and the redistribution of land during the French Revolution as examples *par excellence* of the triumph of administration over government.

Thus in the new society scientific administration will replace political intrigue and government. The various functionaries merely execute the objective dictates of science: 'decisions can only be the result of scientific demonstrations, absolutely independent of all human will'.[5] A residual element of organized social power will be retained for minor police functions, but Saint-Simon's hope is that 'this function of maintaining order can . . . easily become almost entirely a task shared by all citizens'.[6] The strength and cohesiveness generated by this system will render superfluous the need for armed forces either internally or externally, for 'neither princes or people would ever be foolish enough to attack a nation of thirty million men who show no aggressive intention towards their neighbours and who are united among themselves by an excellent scheme based on their interests'.[7] In time, with the inevitable spread of the scheme to other nations, no society would even have the will to attack another. Since this is a society based upon science, the most able will naturally fill the responsible positions. This, however, will not cause resentment, for all will see that it is for the best. The system will also remain capitalist, but with wealth and ownership broadly spread across society.

Saint-Simon sensitively registered the social tendencies of his time; his work both harmonizes the interests of proletariat and bourgeoisie and lays bare the tensions of early industrial capitalism. His work is a complex mixture of technocracy, free-market liberalism and fledgling socialism. Unfortunately, or perhaps fortunately, he died before his unified tendencies went into full-scale battle with one another.

ROBERT OWEN 1771–1858

Robert Owen[8] prided himself on having tested his theories in reality. He was well aware that his reform schemes provoked charges of utopianism, of unreality and unrealizability, but always countered with his experimental results:

> Some of the best intentioned among the various classes in society may still say, 'All this is very delightful and very beautiful in theory, but visionaries alone expect to see it realized.' To this remark only one reply can or ought to be made; that these principles have been carried most success-fully into practice.
> The present Essays [*A New View of Society*] therefore are not brought forward as mere matter of speculation, to amuse the idle visionary who thinks in his closet, and never acts in the world.[9]

The unreality of 'visionaries', however, in terms of social consequences, is negligible when compared with the equally unrealistic, *a priori* dogmatism of religion and political economy, whose powerful adherents defend the indefensible in the teeth of all evidence to the contrary. In his autobiography, Owen drily observes of a hostile clerical neighbour: 'the Rev Mr Menzies had preached in and presided over the town of Lanark for twenty years, and there was no perceptible change for the better among his parishioners';[10] and elsewhere in this work Owen attributes the inadequacies of *laissez-faire* theory to the fact that 'there was not one practical man among the party of political economists'.[11] Owen was quite clear that he was the practical, realistic reformer who had demonstrated a workable future and that it was those who promoted illusions of a religious or political economic nature who were the really dangerous fantasists.

Owen, unlike Saint-Simon, did not ground his alternative in a theory of progressive history. Given what Hazlitt termed his 'one idea', that individuals are created by factors external to themselves, and given that this fact was unknown to all previous generations, then history for Owen is merely the depressing chronicle of humanity's distortion. There is no pattern or direction in history, just different forms of ignorance and misery. As such, its role in social change is the purely negative one of an irrational source of resistance which needs to be overcome. Owen, therefore, sees social transformation in terms of a simple dualism – the bad present (merging imperceptibly into an essentially featureless past) versus the new world of the future. Somehow this future has to be created out of these unpromising materials.

Owen's own experience of the opportunities of early industrial capitalism inclined him to optimism in this matter. If a humble Welsh child could rise to the rank of a successful and fêted industrialist, was not widespread social progress possible? History really did seem to be losing its grip, as the natural and social worlds were transformed. It was indeed possible to see the world as most malleable to the human will. His experience at New Lanark as a reforming manufacturer certainly encouraged this view. The work and domestic conditions of mill workers at this period were sufficiently wretched, and Owen's reforms such a transformation, that he might easily become sanguine about further progress.

Since character was externally determined, the way forward was so to alter the environment as to produce desirable character traits. Autonomous action by the people as a whole was ruled out, as entailing either the untrue philosophical proposition that people formed their own character, or the equally untrue historical proposition that large numbers of people had escaped the effects of a deleterious environment. Only a comparatively rare person like Owen, and initially only Owen, who had, for whatever reason, become conscious of the fundamental principle of character formation, could initiate social reform on the necessarily passive population. The sense of élite social engineering comes out in the formulation of his fundamental principle:

> Any general character from the best to the worst, from the most ignorant to the most enlightened, may be given to any community, even to the world at large, by the application of proper means; which means are to a great extent at the command and under the control of those who have influence in the affairs of men.[12]

In time, however, under the sunny influence of the correct environment, more and more people would become active participants in this process. After Owen's initial hopes of government-led reform had been dashed, his principal strategy became the establishment of alternative communities – villages of co-operation. His experience at New Lanark, always the bedrock of his later work, suggested that it was possible to begin building the new world in the midst of the old. New Lanark was, however, as he acknowledged, only an amelioration of the old system, a compromised adaptation of old institutions to new purposes, and could not be compared with establishing a much more principled structure from scratch. These new institutions, he argued, would co-exist with older structures until the manifest advantages of the co-operative system caused the old to disappear naturally:

> Society did not destroy the old gravel roads before it commenced and completed the railways which were to supersede them. And when the railways were made ready to receive travellers, even the gravel roads were allowed to remain for the use of timid persons, until the old roads were neglected and became evidently useless to the public. In like manner without destroying or injuring the old system of society, the new, with its new divine surroundings, will in every division of it be commenced on new sites, and be made ready to receive willing passengers from the old road or mode of travelling, until the new shall gradually increase to become sufficient to accommodate in a very superior manner the population of the world.[13]

The fact that the actual communities established by Owen and his followers were short-lived should not lead to a glib condemnation of the whole project as 'mere utopianism'. Many of the problems which beset the communities – the nature of property relationships, the question of incentives, relationships with the non-cooperative sector, problems of social cohesion, the existence of freeloaders, conflicts over governmental form and the existence of prior socialization – are questions which all socialist societies have had to and will have to face. Socialists should take care that their rejection of Owen's 'utopian socialism' is not a rejection of socialism itself.

The strategy of establishing islands of socialism in a sea of capitalism had much popular appeal. The villages of co-operation, as well as the other counter-institutions associated with Owenism such as the early co-operatives and unions, encouraged the widespread development of alternative work and domestic arrangements. As E. P. Thompson notes: 'It was not Owen who was "mad", but, from the standpoint of the toilers, [the] social system . . . These men knew from their experience that Owen was sane . . . Owenism was the first of the great social doctrines to grip the imagination of the masses in this period'.[14] A notable example, as Barbara Taylor's path-breaking *Eve and the New Jerusalem* reveals, was the remarkable flowering of the Owenite feminist movement.[15] Furthermore, the complex sociological base of such support belies reductionist claims such as those of Werner Sombart who (speaking of America) stated that 'all socialist utopias come to nothing on roast beef and apple pie'.[16] The whole phenomenon, despite the authoritarian cast of Owen's thought, is an early and instructive example of the principle of prefiguration – namely, that the ends of socialism must be operative in the means.

Despite the many knocks and setbacks he suffered and the growing awareness throughout his long life of the hostility of vested interests to his schemes, he never doubted the possibility of his project. 'Possible' and 'impossible' were subjective judgements and his judgement, he claimed, had proven more reliable than that of his opponents: 'So many impossibilities have been made possible and practical, that the term means only that the thing spoken of is impracticable in the estimation of the person so applying it.'[17] If people called him mad this was simply the scorn and marginality which accompanied advocacy of the new:

> my experience leads me to know that by such kind of madmen, who have sufficient moral courage to disregard public opinion and all the prejudices of their age, the greatest discoveries have been made, and the greatest benefits have been secured for humanity.[18]

Such resolve clearly had its element of naivety. Though he was himself a successful capitalist and a shrewd critic of the antisocial mechanisms of capitalism, Owen did not fully grasp the internal dynamics of the capitalist system. Having no knowledge of the historical development of capitalism, mesmerized as he was by his simplistic theory of environmental determinism, he underestimated the resistances to social change generated by capitalism. Hence his rosy scenario of a painless and inevitable transition to the new world.

CHARLES FOURIER 1772–1837

Fourier[19] considered himself to be the only realistic person in an age of illusion. He knew that the charge of 'utopianism' would result: 'Some readers will cry out "dream", "visionary". Patience! In a short time we will wake them from their own frightful dream, the dream of civilization'.[20] The actual peddlers of utopias, in this pejorative sense, were for Fourier all those contemporary practitioners of the 'inexact' or 'philosophical' sciences – moralists, philosophers, economists, politicians who, through an ignorance of the real world, promised heaven and delivered hell:

> What is Utopia? It is the dream of well-being without the means of execution, without an effective method. Thus all philosophical sciences are Utopias, for they have always led people to the very opposite of the state of well-being they promised them.[21]

The very greatest of the philosophers of the past, such as Plato and Aristotle, used utopianism to puncture the complacency of their contemporaries: 'their utopias were an indirect accusation of the social thought of their age which could not conceive of anything beyond the systems of civilization and barbarism'.[22] They were, however, aware of the limitations of their conceptions. No such modesty characterizes modern savants. Like Saint-Simon, Fourier is particularly critical of the natural rights theories associated with the French Revolution. The abstract claims of liberty, equality and fraternity were confidently trumpeted by the revolutionaries without any appreciation of the substantive changes needed to make these rights a reality. Unaware of the real, immediate causes of the revolution ('it was a competition for sugar and coffee that sent Louis, his family and the élite of France to the Scaffold'),[23] the purveyors of these nostrums were quite powerless to affect events for the better. 'Such was the consequence of the first five years during which the philosophical theories were inflicted on France'.[24]

Fourier rejected the charge of utopianism on the ground that he had discovered the fundamental laws of human existence and was therefore a reliable (in fact *the* only reliable) guide for social reconstruction. According to this new 'Social Science', individuals are naturally attracted to that which is most fulfilling, for God has implanted in humanity a range of sensual, emotional and intellectual passions, whose promptings are inherently beneficial. In this respect Fourier does not square with the widespread belief that 'utopians' invariably base their alternatives on a new human nature fundamentally different from that existing in the societies they wish to transcend. For Fourier, human nature is essentially identical in both the old and the new society: 'the nature of the passions has been and will remain invariable among all nations of men'.[25]

Fourier's achievement was to go beyond Enlightenment clichés on the natural goodness of humanity by radically redefining the good and its origins. He rejected the impoverishment involved in the spiritualization or dematerialization of humanity by giving due importance, for example, to the sensual passions of sight, hearing, touch, smell and taste. This 'radical materialism',[26] as Barthes terms it, made Fourier particularly caustic on those poets and theorists who wished to create idyllic rural utopias out of the miserable existence of supposedly 'natural' peasants. 'I have', he remarked, 'no more faith in the virtues of the shepherds than in those of their apologists'.[27] He was sensitive to the positive dimensions of wealth, not merely in terms of providing the minimum necessities of life, but also as an expression of sensuous/aesthetic impulses. He condemned the ascetic reductionism of the moralists:

> Have they not been trying to persuade us that the diamond is a worthless stone, that gold is a base metal, that sugar and spice are abject and contemptible products, that thatched huts and plain, unvarnished nature are preferable to the palaces of kings?[28]

His advice is clear: 'Search out the tangible wealth, gold, silver, precious metals, jewels and objects of luxury despised by philosophers'.[29] Similarly, he feared that vulgar egalitarianism would lead to a featureless uniformity. Display, and even hierarchy, could be appreciated by all, so long as it was not at the majority's expense:

> Inequality, so much maligned by the philosophers, is not displeasing to men. On the contrary, the bourgeois delights

in hierarchy; he loves to see the bigwigs decked out and parading in their best finery. The poor man views them with the same enthusiasm. Only if he lacks what is necessary does he begin to detest his superiors and the customs of society.[30]

He also displayed great sensitivity to the sexual desires of humanity, causing even a sympathetic critic, at the turn of this century, to note: 'upon this theme he indulges in variations which have proved somewhat embarrassing even to his disciples'.[31] This, it should be observed, was based upon Fourier's somewhat circumspect published works – his then unpublished *The New Amorous World* is much more explicit. Fourier considered all forms of sexual expression to be equally legitimate – not from a liberal toleration perspective but from the conviction that widespread and varied sexual activity was immensely beneficial to human society. Thus he discusses the merits of a whole range of sexual variations (or 'amorous manias' as he terms them), including male and female homosexuality, polygamy, flagellation (both active and passive), voyeurism, 'heel-scratching' and 'hair-plucking' and proclaims his mission to humanity: 'I am . . . going to . . . become the champion of the manias they all have. I am going to teach them to take pride in these secret absurdities which they do not understand and attempt to hide'.[32]

Existing society distorts and mischannels the whole range of potentially creative passions. There is a constant mismatch between passions and functions. This is the root cause of all humanity's miseries. The solution lies in matching passions with functions. Fourier maintained that an immeasurably superior society could be established by letting the passions have free rein within the context of properly organized institutions. Almost any function, no matter how distasteful it might appear to most people, could find devotees. His most famous proposal, in this respect, was 'the Little Hordes', a band of children whose supposed penchant for filth would be utilized in such activities as keeping the sewers in order. In such a society labour would become attractive. One important reason for this is that individuals would not become their functions as in existing society. A person would engage in many activities in one day, thereby gratifying the 'Butterfly' passion, or desire for variation. Fourier outlines the work-day of one citizen, Mondor, who hunts, fishes and studies in the morning, works in the greenhouses and fish-tanks in the afternoon and in the evening joins the sheep-raising group. Such a day would also have its share of aesthetic, sexual and gastronomic gratification. Although Fourier was not free of traditional views of women, the fact that he considered women's oppression to be the barometer of societal oppression and that therefore 'the extension of the privileges of women is the fundamental cause of all social progress'[33] meant that he anticipated their complete emancipation in the new society.

Fourier's speculation on the relationship between humanity and nature in the new society received much ridicule from earlier commentators – these 'mad notions',[34] as Charles Gide put it. Such criticism missed both the enchanting poetry of this vision and Fourier's insightful perception of nature as subject. In the new world social harmony will be echoed throughout the universe. Great climatic improvements will result: the sea will have 'the taste of a kind of lemonade'; new animals, 'antilions', 'antisharks', 'antiseals', friendly to humanity, will emerge; planets will move out of their orbits and communicate with us. Of course there is much that is anthropocentric about all this, but, given its time, it is a remarkable ecological conception. The surrealist André Breton considered Fourier's cosmology to be quite marvellous. Looking back to the earlier writer, Breton enthused – 'He who considered the cherry to be the product of the earth's copulation with itself and the raisin the product of copulation between earth and sun' –[35] and turned on the 'realist' critics of Fourier in an address to the master himself:

> A great atonement is due you; current events are preparing it and might well hasten it . . . Sociology gives itself great airs, proclaiming a little too insistently that it has reached maturity. I do not see how it can justly impute inconsistency and ridiculousness to such works as yours, in which a ceaseless boldness serves an extreme generosity.[36]

The fundamental unit of Fourier's new society was the Phalanx, a predominantly agricultural community (he disliked industrial manufacturing) of approximately 1600 people (derived from his idiosyncratic calculation of the optimum number of main character types). The moment, he felt, was now right for the emergence of these new forms: 'We are on the verge of a great metamorphosis . . . the present is ripe with the future'.[37] His hope was that a rich capitalist, or possibly even the King, would establish the initial community and that its (inevitable) success would stimulate further establishments. That he could maintain such hopes was partly due to the proposed retention of inequalities of wealth and status in the new order. This, of course, raises the problem of potential conflicts of interest, which Fourier did not adequately address. He rather naively believed that devices such as a basic minimum of wealth would remove fundamental socio-economic conflict. He also had little awareness of the problem of conflicting rights, exemplified by his assertion that the astronomer Lalande's peculiar desire to eat live spiders could be legitimately gratified in the new society.

What then is the relationship between the utopian socialists and Marxism? One line of enquiry will be pursued in the next chapter, namely the influence exerted by these theorists on Marx and Engels. We shall also see their influence on later Marxists – as in Marcuse's call for a move from Marx to Fourier. Apart from these actual relationships, there is also a potential relationship. These authors have not been exhausted by the Marxist tradition – contemporary Marxism has much to gain from studying their work. The idea that they have been surpassed, historically superseded, is a piece of foolishness Marxists are particularly prone to. Finally, we should be aware of the question mark placed by the utopian socialists over the science/utopia distinction as it is often understood in Marxism. This latter point is at the heart of the next chapter.

CHAPTER 2

MARX, ENGELS AND UTOPIANISM

The category 'utopian socialism' has often been used in Marxist polemic with little or no idea of its original meaning in the work of Marx and Engels. It is often seen as an encapsulation of the two founders' supposed abhorrence of talking about the future, and is counterposed to something called 'scientific socialism' which is apparently concerned only with the past and the present. A whole range of other connotations have become attached to this sad little dualism – unreality, error and subjectivity on one side; realism, truth and objectivity on the other. Marx and Engels, in contrast, did not object to anticipation as such, and clearly engaged in it themselves; they had the greatest respect for Owen, Fourier and Saint-Simon, though not for most of these thinkers' disciples; they also, in the main, had no time for the positivist concept of science implied in the distinction with utopia. To show this it will be necessary to trace the development of their work.

Before the beginning of their life-long association in the latter half of 1844, it was the work of Engels rather than of Marx which concerned itself the more explicitly with utopianism. More accurately, Engels' work in the early 1840s displayed a concern with socialism/communism, for the category of 'utopian socialism' lay in the future – the work of Owen, Fourier and Saint-Simon (along with that of, for example, Cabet and Proudhon) was socialism, and whatever the basis of Engels' criticism of these thinkers in this period, it was not a rejection of their enterprise as utopian. Writing in the Owenite journal *The New Moral World* in 1843, his respect for 'the bright sparks of genius . . . in Saint-Simon . . . and some of his disciples'[1] and the 'mighty intellect'[2] of Fourier is apparent. Of the two, his preference is for

22

the 'scientific' Fourier with his 'scientific research, cool, unbiased, systematic thought; in short *social philosophy*; whilst Saint-Simonism can only be called social poetry'.[3] It is not just that Engels takes these thinkers' critiques seriously; he also takes equally seriously their project of establishing alternative societies. Thus Fourier is criticized not for the idea of Phalansteres but for his retention of private property in these new institutions. In a speech at Elberfeld (shortly after he had begun his collaboration with Marx), Engels explicitly endorsed aspects of Owen's vision of future society: 'Here', he said, 'I should like to subscribe to the proposals of Robert Owen, the English [*sic*] Socialist, since these are the most practical and most fully worked out'.[4] In an article, he highlights the feasibility of the Owenite and other communal schemes: 'For communism, social existence and activity based on community of goods is not only possible but has actually been realised in many communities in America and in one place in England with the greatest success'.[5] Or again, with respect to the followers of Cabet: 'the French Icarian Communists are estimated at about half a million in number, women and children not taken into account [*sic*]. A pretty respectable phalanx, isn't it?'.[6] In the speech at Elberfeld he displayed, on the question of the transition to communism, no qualms about these utopian perspectives:

> There are various ways to this end; the English will probably begin by setting up a number of colonies and leaving it to every individual whether to join or not; the French, on the other hand, will be likely to prepare and implement communism on a national basis.[7]

As we saw in the case of Fourier, Engels was not uncritical of these thinkers. In particular, his perception of class and class conflict made him highly sceptical about aspects of their work, but there is no suggestion that he considered these thinkers anything less than central, and certainly not marginal or alien, to a successful socialist strategy.

Engels brought this perspective into his relationship with Marx. In a letter of early 1845, Engels informs Marx of his plan to publish a library 'of the best foreign socialist writers. Fourier would seem to be the best to start off with'.[8] Returning to this project in a subsequent letter, he reveals his dislike of the more exotic elements of Fourier ('I wanted Fourier – omitting of course the cosmogenic nonsense')[9] and implies a unity between his own ideas and those of Marx and an affinity between these and aspects of utopian socialism. He wished 'to start off with the things which have most to offer to the Germans and are closest to our principles; the best that is, of Fourier, Owen, the Saint-Simonists, etc.'.[10] What then was the perspective on 'utopian socialism' brought by Marx to the relationship?

In a pioneering article in 1948, Georges Gurvitch[11] argued the case for Saint-Simon's influence on the young Marx, pointing to the various encounters Marx had with Saint-Simonian currents and the affinity between some of the ideas in the two thinkers. With respect to these affinities, Gurvitch mentions the importance of historical development, class, work and the study of the social whole to Marx and Saint-Simon, as well as the shared notion of the replacement of government by administration. Hopefully, the account of Saint-Simon in the previous chapter will help to underline Gurvitch's argument. Saint-Simon's social philosophy is certainly, in a number of respects, a remarkable anticipation of Marx.

Long before he became a socialist in 1843, Marx had come into contact with socialist, particularly Saint-Simonian, ideas. The liberal milieu in which he grew up in the Rhineland was sympathetic to French Enlightenment thought, and through his friendship with the veteran radical aristocrat, Ludwig von Westphalen (his future father-in-law), he was introduced to the work of Saint-Simon. At Berlin University as both Blumenberg[12] and Bottomore[13] have pointed out, he was influenced by a law lecturer, Edward Gans, whose Saint-Simonianism clearly emerges in an 1836 work which strikingly anticipates phraseology in *The Manifesto of the Communist Party*:

> the Saint-Simonians have said something of importance and have put their finger on a public scandal of the day . . . Once there was the opposition between master and slave, then between patrician and plebeian, and later still between feudal lord and vassal; now we have the idle rich and the worker.[14]

Gurvitch sees Gans' attempt to combine Saint-Simon and Hegel as part of a general Saint-Simonian influence on the German Young Hegelians (Feuerbach, Bruno Bauer, Ruge, Hess, etc.) and argues 'that Marx's deep knowledge of the writings of Saint-Simon and Saint-Simonism dates from this period'.[15] One early example of this influence is in the *Critique of Hegel's Philosophy of Right* (1843), where Marx refers to a perennial feature of his vision of future society, the end of the state, and hints at its Saint-Simonian origins. It occurs in a discussion of the relationship between democracy and the state, where Marx remarks: 'The French have recently interpreted this as meaning that in true democracy the political state is annihilated'.[16] It surely cannot be maintained, as Ryazanoff claimed in the 1920s, that 'Saint-Simon's influence was small upon Marx'[17] (though even he grudgingly concedes Saint-Simon's 'anticipation' of the 'abolition of the state') and even that 'Saint-Simon's philosophy and his historical theories could not have exercised an influence on Marx'.[18] Turning to other 'utopian' influences: it is possible that Marx came into contact with Fourier's ideas in his home town of Trier, via the Fourierist Secretary to the Council, Ludwig Gall, and, in Avineri's[19] opinion, Marx probably read Lorenz von Stein's influential study of French socialism and communism shortly after its publication in 1842.

Marx's flowering as a socialist/communist occurred in the radical climate of Paris after his move there in late 1843. For the first couple of weeks, he and Jenny Marx lived in a small-scale quasi-Fourierist 'phalanstry' organized by Arnold Ruge, which incorporated a number of aspects of communal living. In Paris, Marx encountered the flesh-and-blood proletariat and absorbed himself in their theory and practice. To Feuerbach he enthused: 'you would have to attend one of the meetings of the French workers to appreciate the pure freshness, the nobility which burst forth from these toil-worn men'.[20] In the same letter he quoted a Fourierist work to exemplify the difference between practical/materialist French socialism and the theoretical/idealist concern of the Germans: 'Do not these sentences give the impression that the Frenchman has deliberately set his passion against the pure activity of German thought? One does not think in order to think, etc.'.[21] A whole range of other radical thinkers received Marx's admiration in this period, including some he would later denounce in characteristically strong terms. He wrote, for example, in 1844: 'I call to mind Weitling's brilliant writings, which as regards theory are often superior even to those of Proudhon, however much they are inferior to the latter in their execution'.[22] It was in this context that Marx began his collaboration with Engels in late 1844.

The initial product of this collaboration was the turgid *The Holy Family*. Although 'collaborative', Engels and Marx wrote distinct sections (the bulk by Marx) of this critique of the Bauer brothers and their 'critical criticism'. Owen, Fourier and Saint-Simon receive a number of favourable mentions from Marx. He refers to the materialism of Owen and Fourier, highlights Proudhon's debt to Fourier and Saint-Simon, speaks of 'Fourier's masterly characterisation'[23] of marriage and, in a passage that anticipates *The German Ideology*, attacks Bruno Bauer's conception of the 'rights of man':

> compared to his discovery that the rights of man are not 'inborn' – a discovery which has been made innumerable times in England during the last 40-odd years – Fourier's assertion that the right to fish, to hunt, etc., are inborn rights of men is one of genius.[24]

This work is part of the gradual emergence of the various elements of Marxism: Marx and Engels' synthesis of left-Hegelianism, critical political economy and, of course, utopian socialism, the three 'sources' and 'component parts' of Marxism, as Lenin put it.[25] In the process, Marx and Engels were not entirely fair to the great 'utopians'. Their perception that they were creating something radical and new caused them at times to understate and even caricature the achievements of Saint-Simon, Owen and Fourier.

The category 'utopian socialism' was a product of Marx and Engels' growing involvement in working-class politics. Their encounter with the politics of Fourierism, Owenism and Saint-Simonianism forced them to think hard about the relationship between the founders of these schools and their latter-day disciples. In *The German Ideology* (1846), a historical materialist framework is provided. These initial systems 'appeared in the early days of the communist movement' and 'corresponded perfectly to the still undeveloped consciousness of the proletarians, who were then just beginning to play an active part'.[26] In changed circumstances, however, orthodoxy can become reactionary: 'Fourier's orthodox disciples of the *Démocratie pacifique* . . . are, for all their orthodoxy doctrinaire bourgeois, the very antipodes of Fourier'.[27] The strengths of a system necessarily reflect the conditions of the time:

> All epoch-making systems have as their real content the needs of the time in which they arose. Each one of them is based on the whole of the antecedent development of a nation, on the historical growth of its class relations, with their political, moral, philosophical and other consequences.[28]

The task was, therefore, to develop a politics appropriate to the time. Marx and Engels deemed as inappropriate the positing of utopias not grounded in existing tendencies. Thus Engels took the English Owenite socialists to task for doing precisely this: 'They acknowledge no historic development and wish to place the nation in a state of Communism at once, overnight, without pursuing the political struggle to the end, at which it dissolves itself'.[29] Paul Annekov graphically described Marx's confrontation with Weitling in early 1846 over the question of the way forward:

> Marx's sarcastic speech boiled down to this: to rouse the population without giving them any firm, well-thought-out reasons for their activity would be simply to deceive them. The raising of fantastic hopes just spoken of, Marx continued, led only to the final ruin and not to the saving of the sufferers. To call to the workers without any strictly scientific ideas or constructive doctrine, especially in Germany, was equivalent to vain dishonest play at preaching which assumed on the one side an inspired prophet and on the other only gaping asses.[30]

What is under attack here is not anticipation as such, but rather the failure to root this anticipation in a theoretical framework cognizant of the essential dynamics of capitalism. This in turn had to be based in, and draw sustenance from, those social forces which were destroying the old society and ushering in the new, which, for Marx and Engels, meant becoming a part of the proletarian movement.

Apart from Saint-Simon's socio-history there is also a German idealist pedigree for this type of analysis, one which is very much to the fore in Marx's early theoretical work. Hegel had criticized Fichte for his one-sided stress on autonomous subjectivity – on the supremacy of the 'ought' in his system. 'Fichte', he said, 'is stuck fast on an ought to be'.[31] The objective dimension is inadequately recognized. In the *Phenomenology of Spirit*, Hegel argues for the interpenetration of 'ought' and 'is':

> What is universally valid is also universally effective; what *ought* to be, in fact also *is*, and what only *ought* to be without [actually] being, has no truth. The instinct of Reason, for its part, rightly holds firmly to this standpoint, and refuses to be led astray by figments of thought which only *ought* to be and

as 'oughts', are credited with truth, although they are
nowhere met with in experience.[32]

In his leftist, materialist reading of Hegel, the young Marx
develops the notion of the interaction of subject/object, ought/is
in the historical process. The issue is not the future versus the
present, but that the future be grounded in the present. This is
the perspective from which Marx and Engels' strictures on
anticipation should be seen.

They saw *The Manifesto of the Communist Party* (1848), which
drew together the strands of their previous work, as a
contribution to the collective conscious-raising of the proletariat.
One important task was to provide a guide to the various
socialisms on offer, and it is in this context that they produced
their first systematic analysis of what they now termed 'Critical-
Utopian Socialism and Communism'. The main elements of
their analysis were:

1 Utopian socialism emerged at a time when the class struggle
  between bourgeoisie and proletariat was undeveloped.
2 Although aware of the divided and unstable nature of
  capitalism it could, of necessity, see no potential in the infant
  proletariat. The proletariat was simply the most suffering class.
3 As a consequence: 'Social action is to yield to their personal
  inventive action, historically created conditions of emancipation to fantastic ones, and the gradual class organisation of the
  proletariat to an organisation of society specially contrived by
  these inventors'.[33]
4 The utopians saw themselves as champions of all humanity,
  above classes and their struggles.
5 Since their goals were in everybody's interests there was
  nothing to be lost, and much to be gained, in seeking ruling
  class support.
6 Success was, therefore, dependent on the peaceful methods
  of example and persuasion.

The problem for these pioneers was not that they looked
forward, but that this occurred at a time when the future and the
steps to it were necessarily opaque. Blame is reserved for those
who can know better – utopian socialists in the era of the
developed proletariat:

  although the originators of these systems were, in many
  respects, revolutionary, their disciples have, in every case,

formed mere reactionary sects. They hold fast by the original views of their masters, in opposition to the progressive historical development of the proletariat.[34]

Marx and Engels underline the critical element in the early utopian socialists and maintain that it still has continuing validity: 'They attack every principle of existing society. Hence they are full of the most valuable materials for the enlightenment of the working class'.[35] Although hinting here at their own debt to the likes of Saint-Simon, Owen and Fourier, the clear objective of the section on the utopian socialists in the *Manifesto* is to make this tradition unattractive to potential recruits. This is another reason for the element of distortion that crept into Marx and Engels' account of the 'utopian socialists'. Their desire to stress the political distinctiveness of their own stance led them to be less than fair to their 'utopian' predecessors.

The similarity between Marx and Engels' characterization of communist society and that of the utopian socialists could have escaped no-one. Neither here, nor elsewhere, do they deny these similarities. However, they saw their dispute as methodological; the utopian socialist vision is at best a subjective imaginative abstraction from the divisions of class society, whilst the communist vision, by contrast, is the objective *telos* capitalist society creates as it negates itself. From this perspective, particularly in subsequent works and especially when there was no pressing political need to hammer the utopian socialists, the utopian pioneers were seen as immensely perceptive and talented individuals – creators of work in which 'there is the anticipation and imaginative expression of a new world'.[36] They simply were not, and could not be, anything more than this.

Marx and Engels' ambivalent relationship to Owen, Fourier and Saint-Simon haunts their mature work. In Marx's case the most graphic example occurs in the difference between his first draft of *The Civil War in France* (1871) and the final published version. In the initial draft he repeats the historical materialist placing of the utopians and then relates their vision to the events of the Paris Commune:

> The Utopian founders of sects . . . [described] . . . the goal of the social movement, the supersession of the wages system with all its economical conditions of class rule . . . From the moment the working men's class movement became real the fantastic utopias evanesced – not because the working class

had given up the end aimed at by these Utopians, but because they had found the real means to realise them – but in their place came a real insight into the historical conditions of the movement and a more and more gathering force of the militant organisation of the working class. But the last two ends of the movement proclaimed by the Utopians are the last ends proclaimed by the Paris Revolution and by the International. Only the means are different and the real conditions of the movement are no longer clouded in utopian fables.[37]

In the published version, however, this is dropped and a stark attack on utopianism, often quoted in characterizations of Marx as an anti-utopian, is inserted: 'The working class . . . have no ready-made utopias to introduce . . . They have no ideals to realise, but to set free the elements of the new society with which old collapsing society itself is pregnant'.[38] Engels, too, was always to acknowledge a link between Marxism and the utopians, though often couched in the vagueness of metaphor, as in 1874 when he said of Marxism that 'it rests on the shoulders of Saint-Simon, Fourier and Owen'[39] or, in a preface to *Socialism: Utopian and Scientific* (1882), where he proclaimed that 'we German socialists are proud of the fact that we are descendants . . . of Saint-Simon, Fourier and Owen'[40] (he also acknowledges a descent from Kant, Fichte and Hegel).

It is worth pausing momentarily to look at this latter work of Engels. It was extracted from a larger polemical work against Eugen von Dühring and was originally entitled *Die Entwicklung des Sozialismus von der Utopie zur Wissenschaft* (the development, or even evolution, of socialism from utopia to science). The contrast with its English title, *Socialism: Utopian and Scientific*, is significant – the former suggesting Marx and Engels' historical materialist analysis of utopianism, whereas the latter implies a sharp dualism of world-views; one true, one false. Engels himself must bear some of the responsibility for the possibility of such a shift, with his paeans to science and odd materialist metaphysics – and Marx too has passages with a distinctly scientistic cast. However, the idea of a 'scientific socialism', which somehow reflected, and was legitimized by, the inexorable march of history, is alien to their dialectical perspective. Genuine socialism is a part of the process of emancipation and not an external reflection of it. Socialist theory analyses and assesses, articulates and identifies itself with, the proletariat's freeing of humanity *from* blind historical forces. As Marcuse noted: 'There can be no blind necessity in tendencies that terminate in a free and self-conscious society . . . Not the slightest natural necessity or automatic inevitability guarantees the transition from capitalism to socialism'.[41] Marx and Engels had not criticized the utopian socialists' 'search after a new social science, after new social laws',[42] merely to put in its place a new tyrannical 'science'. None the less, the concepts – and the ambiguities – were there for a very different interpretation.

How are the various images of socialism/communism outlined in the *Critique of the Gotha Programme* and elsewhere to be fitted into this perspective? For Marx and Engels the shared life-experience of the working class, its experience of exploitation, tended to generate alternatives, and it was possible for socialist theoreticians, on the basis of insight into the whole, to perceive, generalize and elaborate this experience and then represent it back to the proletariat for consolidation; hence the images of emancipated society in Marx and Engels' own work. Throughout, the autonomy of the working class had to be respected, for 'the emancipation of the working classes must be conquered by the working classes themselves'.[43] The proletariat's experience of capitalism was constantly changing and with it its perceptions of the future. Old scenarios, therefore, had to be ruthlessly discarded when they were no longer appropriate, lest they foreclose the future. Democratic structures would help to ensure this. In this way the twin evils of relativism and tailism on the one hand and authoritarian vanguardism on the other would, hopefully, be overcome. The process of communism would then occur:

> Communism is for us not a state of affairs which is to be established, an ideal to which reality will have to adjust itself. We call communism the real movement which abolishes the present state of things. The conditions of this movement result from the now existing premise.[44]

Marx and Engels were highly sensitive to the necessary element of unpredictability in the future and some of their most negative remarks on utopianism occur in this context. Since socialism entails autonomy, socialist behaviour will be characterized by its diversity and spontaneity. From the perspective of the future the speculation of earlier times will inevitably seem wide of the mark. As Engels noted:

Once such people appear, they will not care a rap about what we today think they should do. They will establish their own practice and their own public opinion, conformable therewith, on the practice of each individual – and that's the end of it.[45]

By contrast with socialism, it is capitalism's denial of autonomy which makes *its* future so transparent.

It is in this context that Marx's comments on future speculation contained in a letter to Domela Nieuwenhuis (1881) should be understood. In this letter he argues that the French Revolution of 1789 could in no way be seen as the outcome in practice of earlier speculation: 'had', he asks, 'any eighteenth-century Frenchman the faintest idea beforehand, *a priori*, of the manner in which the demands of the French bourgeoisie would be forced through?'[46] This observation leads immediately into the proposition that revolutionary anticipation distracts from immediate tasks: 'The doctrinaire and inevitably fantastic anticipation of the programme of action for a revolution of the future only diverts one from the struggle of the present'.[47] 'Scientific insight' into, and the fact of, capitalism's self-destruction should be the bedrock of the revolutionary – post-revolutionary society can be left to the denizens of that time: 'as soon as a real proletarian revolution breaks out the conditions of its immediately next *modus operandi* . . . will be in existence'.[48]

Marx and Engels subjected their own remarks on future society to this sharp historical scrutiny. Their verdict in 1872 on the anticipations in the *Manifesto* was: 'no special stress is laid on the revolutionary measures proposed at the end of Section II. That passage would in many respects, be very differently worded today . . . this programme has in some details become antiquated'.[49] This was due to the changed experience of the proletariat. Massive industrial development had stimulated greater self-organization by the class and there was 'the practical experience gained, first in the February Revolution, and then still more in the Paris Commune, where the proletariat for the first time held political power for two whole months'.[50]

Having said this, however, certain constants do characterize the two thinkers' vision of communism. There is undoubtedly a strong negative element in this vision, the absence of a whole range of capitalist features (the abolition of A, the disappearance of B, the removal of C), and this has generated the argument that Marx and Engels are mainly concerned with what communism isn't rather than with what it is. Concern with the present and its destruction is clearly central to the Marxist project, and its debt to Hegelian dialectics is reflected in the image of the negation of capitalism. None the less, the conception of communism as the 'negation of the negation' is neither nihilist nor simply negative but implies a transformational synthesis, a concept which itself requires some prior notion of the good or desirable. A positive image of future life underpins Marx and Engels' talk of 'the negative' and here, as elsewhere, the influence of the utopian socialists can be detected. On a number of occasions Marx and Engels strongly hint at this influence. We have already mentioned Marx's reference to the French origins of 'the withering away of the state'. Engels specifically relates this concept to Saint-Simon in *Socialism: Utopian and Scientific*:

> In 1816 he [Saint-Simon] declared that politics was the science of production and foretold the complete absorption of politics by economics . . . What is already very plainly expressed is the transition from political rule over men to the administration of things and the guidance of the processes of production – that is to say, the 'abolition of the state', about which there has recently been so much noise.[51]

The idea of the destruction of the distinction between town and country repeatedly appears in their work connected with the names of Owen and Fourier. That Marx may have obtained his picture of the multi-faceted communist from Fourier, as referred to earlier, receives further evidence from Engels who links Fourier with Owen as anticipators of the abolition of the division of labour:

> within agriculture as well as industry both of them . . . demand the greatest possible variety of occupation for each individual, and in accordance with this the training of the youth for the utmost possible all-round technical functions. They both consider that man should gain universal development through universal practical activity and that labour should recover the attractiveness of which the division of labour has despoiled it, in the first place through this variation of occupation, and through the correspondingly short duration of the 'sitting' – to use Fourier's expression – devoted to each particular kind of work.[52]

Marx, in the *Grundrisse*, although distancing himself from what he, mistakenly, takes to be Fourier's conception of attractive labour ('This does not mean that labour can be made merely a joke, or amusement, as Fourier naively expressed it.'),[53] does it in a context suggestive of Fourier's influence. Other areas of influence include Fourier's views on the emancipation of women and the abolition of the bourgeois family and Owen's pioneering work on communist organization. Clearly, there were many more influences than the utopian socialists and the whole vision is much more than the sum of these influences. From the fragments scattered throughout Marx and Engels' work an impressive utopia can be assembled, as Bertell Ollman has done in a reconstruction of what he terms 'the most famous of utopias and among the least known'.[54] This utopia easily matches in imaginative power and profundity of conception the great utopias of western thought, though its authors, for reasons which should now be clear, never crafted it into a comprehensive whole.

Marx and Engels thus left an ambiguous legacy in which vigorous attacks on utopianism accompanied clear utopian speculation. So long as capitalism developed along classic Marxist lines, the questions of internal differentiations in the consciousness of the proletariat and of the relationship between proletarian class consciousness and the perspectives of those 'bourgeois ideologists' who had gone over to the proletariat, whilst important, were not of major significance. However, once capitalism began to mutate in various ways, the whole issue of conflicting visions moved to the centre of the stage. This was also the case in countries not yet fully on the capitalist road, such as in Russia, where the diversity of class was matched by a diversity of vision.

CHAPTER 3

THE SECOND INTERNATIONAL

The principal theoreticians of the Second International prided themselves on the scientific nature of their socialism. In this age of technology and of Darwin, the aspiration to be scientific was widespread. In the work of Marx and Engels, their latter-day followers found the ideal concept to describe those not in a scientific state of grace – 'utopian'. This concept they wielded like a club both against ideological foes and against each other. Utopianism was a mortal sin. This general, indiscriminate use of the term partly arose from, and partly contributed to, the feeling that there was something wrong in speculating about the future. Such speculation was viewed as somehow arbitrary and abstract, against the 'laws and facts' spirit of the age. Certainly, as we have seen, it was possible to read Marx and Engels in a way that gave credence to such a view. And yet these thinkers found it quite impossible to do without a future orientation. In the complex world of the late nineteenth century, Marxists, like everybody else, felt the need for both long and short term speculation. This had to be achieved, however, without committing the sin of utopianism. As we shall see, this task caused them many problems.

In this chapter we shall look at two sets of three thinkers: one group of thinkers connected with the leading party of the International, the German Social Democratic Party; the other consisting of members of the fledgling Russian movement. This is not an arbitrary choice, for out of these two centres emerged the two dominant currents of twentieth century socialism – social democracy and communism. The choice of three thinkers in each case reflects the major tensions within the movement. Three broad currents can be isolated. Orthodox thinkers like

Kautsky (1854–1938) and Plekhanov (1856–1918) tended to assert the continuing validity of the classic 'breakdown of capitalism' scenario (as they understood it to exist) in Marx and Engels' writings, though this is not to suggest that they were mere rigid dogmatists. The revisionists, Bernstein (1850–1932) and Kuskova (1869–1959), developed a reformist politics on the claim that recent developments in capitalism had fatally undermined aspects of the Marxist system. The radicals, Luxemburg (1871–1919) and Lenin (1870–1924), although they bitterly attacked revisionism and rallied to the support of orthodoxy, did so in a way which recognized that times had indeed radically changed and that a revolutionary Marxism needed to adapt accordingly. Such differences are important in understanding the various approaches to future speculation.

KAUTSKY, BERNSTEIN AND LUXEMBURG

For Kautsky, capitalism was inexorably negating itself. His work abounds with references to the 'necessity', the 'inevitability' of socialism. This does not, however, generate a complacent, fatalistic perspective, either at the level of theory or at the level of practice, as his constant interventions in the politics of the time reveal. Rather it legitimates, on the one hand, polemic against perspectives not scientifically grounded, and, on the other, the possibility of genuine scientific anticipation. In the case of the former, he himself attacked both the revisionists (for their false interpretations of capitalism) and the Austro-Marxists (for their attempt to import abstract, ahistorical Kantianism into Marxism). All this testifies to his belief that the proletariat is not an automatic force and that it can be delayed from fulfilling its historic mission. Sound theory (including sound goals) is essential. However, like the other thinkers in this section, he does inherit Marx and Engels' fear that the future should not be foreclosed, that the future would be the creation of the people of that time and would necessarily differ from the speculations of earlier seers. His assertion at one time that the question of the dictatorship of the proletariat could be 'tranquilly left to the future'[1] is meant to be in the spirit of this injunction. None the less, he was quite unable – and unwilling – to do without goals.

In *Thomas More and His Utopia*, Kautsky spells out his belief in the far-sighted individual:

But a thinker who takes his stand on the material conditions may be a whole epoch in advance of his time, if he
perceives a newly evolving mode of production and its social
consequences not only sooner than most of his contemporaries, but straining far into the future, also glimpses the
more rational mode of production into which it will develop.[2]

Although he refers here specifically to More, this perspective
does inform his general approach to socialist politics. Though
still committed to the proposition that the working class must
emancipate itself, there is great emphasis in Kautsky's work on
the need for scientific leadership. This leadership, as Salvadori
points out, is not seen as being identical to political leadership,
for the former will emerge from bourgeois strata whilst the latter
must come from the working class.[3] The distinction could,
however, easily disappear into an intellectual vanguardist
conception, as can be seen in the alacrity with which Lenin
pounced on Kautsky's idea. Lenin quoted, in *What is to be done?*,
these 'profoundly true and important words' of Karl Kautsky:

But socialism and the class struggle arise side by side and
not one out of the other; each arises under different
conditions. Modern socialist consciousness can arise only on
the basis of profound scientific knowledge . . . The vehicle of
science is not the proletariat, but the bourgeois intelligentsia:
it was in the minds of individual members of this stratum that
modern socialism originated, and it was they who
communicated it to the more intellectually developed
proletarians who in turn, introduce it into the proletarian
class struggle where conditions allow that to be done. This
socialist consciousness is something introduced into the
proletarian class struggle from without and not something
that arose within it spontaneously.[4]

Socialism is therefore, in some mysterious fashion, to be
distilled from objective scientific laws and then injected into the
proletariat – a conception diametrically opposed to Marx's own.
Clearly, goals assume a whole new purpose and importance in
this theory. 'What the workers ask of the academics', Kautsky
argues, 'is knowledge of the goal'.[5] Goals are the compass
points in the disorientating terrain of modern capitalism: the
supposed general will amidst the merely contingent wills of
individual proletarians. And yet, because he saw science as

opposed to utopia, he oscillates between implicit and explicit discussion of goals and dire warnings about the dangers of futuristic blueprints. Thus, in *The Social Revolution*, in a section entitled 'On the day after the social revolution', he says that this is not

> a return to Utopianism . . . I am thoroughly convinced that it is not our task to invent recipes for the kitchens of the future, and when more than ten years ago the German Social Democracy proposed to include in its program demands for such measures as would accelerate the transformation from a capitalist to a socialist manner of production. I opposed this. . . . But I maintain that it is a help to political clearness to examine the problems that will grow out of the conquest of political power by us.[6]

Like Marx, therefore, he displays an anti-utopian utopianism, but in a way criticized by Marx in the *Theses on Feuerbach* since it seeks to 'divide society into two parts, one of which is superior to society'.[7]

This fear of future speculation was a simple fact of life in Kautsky's party – the SPD. Peter Nettl has argued that, in the SPD, discussion of post-revolutionary society was one of the 'universally respected taboos' and points out by way of illustration that, between 1882 and 1914, the party journal *Neue Zeit* (edited by Kautsky) contained only *one* article dealing with future society and that this was Kautsky's own discussion of *past* millenarian societies.[8] In the same vein, David Lovell quotes Masaryk's reminiscences that, in an international journal devoting a special issue to future society, 'Liebknecht [an SPD leader] almost facetiously refuses to depict the future socialist order'[9] and that, in a debate on the same theme in the German Imperial Diet in 1893, 'the socialist deputies, Liebknecht, Bebel, and others treated the theme lightly'.[10] If this is taken to mean that there was in the SPD a climate antithetical to developed, self-conscious discussion of what was to replace capitalism, then this point is incontrovertible. Such an approach played into the hands of the opposition. Socialists could be portrayed as destroyers of an order they had no replacement for, a problem Kautsky was aware of, arguing in *The Social Revolution* that some thought on post-revolutionary society 'is also valuable for propaganda since our opponents frequently assert that our victory will give us unsoluble problems'.[11] Bismarck mocked Bebel with an invitation to an evening's conversation where he 'would hope at last to learn how Herr Bebel and his comrades really imagine the state of the future for which they would prepare us by tearing down all that exists, that we cherish, and that protects us'.[12] The approach also ignored the immense appetite for utopian speculation manifested in the overwhelming success of the German translation of Bellamy's *Looking Backward*. The right had no such qualms and rapidly filled the vacuum with cheap novels portraying the hell of future socialist society and, even more sinisterly, developing utopian visions of strong leaders, international power and racial purity. The left thus abandoned this great reservoir of utopianism to be poisoned by the right.

What cannot be held against Kautsky, however, is the old charge that his was a fatalistic Marxism passively waiting for the proletarian *deus ex machina* to deliver the millennium and that this led to the collapse of German Social Democracy (and the Second International) in the face of the world war. Echoes of this are to be found in Kolakowski's claim that Kautskyite 'centrism' 'was a philosophy of indecision and was incapable of taking up a clear position on questions that had to be decided'.[13] Even Lenin, in his vitriolic *The Proletarian Revolution and the Renegade Kautsky*, does not make this charge – a not particularly surprising fact given Kautsky's presence in *What is to be done?*. The tossing of insults between Kautsky and the Bolsheviks in the wake of the Soviet revolution was in terms of different conceptions of the transition to socialism: Kautsky charged the Bolsheviks with – surprise, surprise – 'utopianism' in wishing to introduce socialism overnight in a backward country, whilst Lenin maintained that Kautsky fetishized bourgeois democracy. It was not part of Lenin's case that Kautsky was a passive fatalist.

It is true to say, however, that Kautsky's Marxism did suffer from that fear of utopianism so characteristic of the Second International. Unable to do without a future, but unwilling to linger in such forbidden territory, the end results were inevitably half-hearted and were clearly seen as such by perceptive contemporaries. Thus Karl Korsch, writing in 1920, pointed to the bland and unimaginative nature of Kautsky's speculation, its lack of 'the creative fantasy of a revolutionary who has already carried out the transformation from the old to the new in his thought'.[14] Korsch continued:

And from the fact that Kautsky and all of those who stand close to him do not possess such creative, faithful revolutionary fantasy we can explain their all too long denial of practical future-oriented thoughts. From this lack of revolutionary fantasy we may also explain the ghostliness of the programs of action and the plans for socialization – pale and genuinely sufficient for no one, least of all satisfactory to the striving masses – which these people . . . developed.[15]

Korsch also shrewdly put his finger on the root cause of all this – the obsessive and ill-conceived science/utopia distinction with which the Second International operated:

throughout this entire period . . . of the Second International, the majority of spokesmen of revolutionary socialism sought to guarantee the 'scientific' character of the Marxian doctrine by rejecting from the beginning every attempted clarification of the following question as a relapse into pre-Marxian ideology and utopianism: How on the basis of each economic and social-psychological stage of development, can the socialistic demand 'socialization of the means of production' be practically realized?[16]

In short, adherence to a narrow, positivistic conception of 'scientific socialism' clearly blunted the cutting edge of Kautsky's Marxism – a failure that could only be compounded by his 'scientific leadership' approach, for if you must have founts of science they should at least have imagination.

Bernstein's revisionist critique posed a fundamental threat to Kautsky's perspective by challenging the orthodox scenario of capitalism's self-destruction. Part of a jotting on the back of an envelope, found in Bernstein's papers after his death, pithily expresses this challenge: 'Peasants do not sink; middle class does not disappear; crises do not grow ever larger; misery and serfdom do not increase'.[17] Capitalism was developing in new directions: ownership of property and shares was becoming more widespread; small and medium agriculture was on the increase; wages were rising and general prosperity was growing. An increasingly complex class system gave the lie to orthodox anticipations of intensifying class polarization.

As the old certainties could no longer be maintained, argued Bernstein, Marxists should take a long, hard look at the supposed terminus of history: the traditional image of the revolutionary transition to socialism, grounded in those certainties. This involved a twofold process: firstly it was necessary to take note of the ways in which capitalism had developed since Marx and Engels had formulated their conceptions (in other words, to bring the theory up to date); secondly, and more painfully, it involved recognizing the 'residue of utopianism in the Marxist system',[18] that 'Hegelian' apriorism which seduced Marx away from the scientific study of society and which resulted in the imposition of an arbitrary pattern upon the future. Marx, he says,

> has raised a mighty building within the framework of a
> scaffolding he found existing, and in its erection he kept
> strictly to the laws of scientific architecture as long as they
> did not collide with the conditions which the construction of
> the scaffolding prescribed, but he neglected or evaded them
> when the scaffolding did not allow of their observance.
> Where the scaffolding put limits in the way of the
> building, instead of destroying the scaffolding he changed
> the building itself at the cost of its right proportions and so
> made it all the more dependent on the scaffolding.[19]

This is the background to his (in)famous remark 'that the movement means everything for me and that what is usually called "the final aim of socialism" is nothing'.[20] In one respect he is merely repeating here Marx's own fears about foreclosing the future, that new factors will constantly spring up which could never be fully anticipated. He is, however, also arguing that, given the changes capitalism has undergone, Marx's scenario of the establishment of socialism has, so to speak, lost its locomotive and with it its validity. In its place, Bernstein proposes a concern with the here and now which eschews any detailed speculation on the future:

> I have at no time had an excessive interest in the future,
> beyond general principles; I have not been able to read to the
> end any picture of the future. My thoughts and efforts are
> concerned with the duties of the present and the nearest
> future, and I only busy myself with the perspectives beyond
> so far as they give me a line of conduct for suitable action
> now.[21]

What this meant in practice was a commitment to reformism – not, in fact, the rejection of vision, but rather the adoption of the scaled-down vision of social democracy. Via a logical non-sequitur, therefore, Bernstein turned his attack on 'utopianism' into the promotion of his own reformist utopia. In so doing he was merely registering the actual development of the German Social Democratic Party. Kautsky preserved the memory of Marx's vision, but the party as a whole was revisionist to the core. As Trotsky noted, 'the everyday reformist struggle had acquired a self-sufficient character while the final goal was kept in Kautsky's department'.[22] Events were tragically to reveal the unrealities of revisionist utopianism.

One response to the revisionist critique was to dig one's heels in, deny the evidence and thereby protect the integrity of Marx and Engels' system. There was a strong dose of this in Kautsky's approach. Revisionism threatened the entire conception of scientific leadership by putting a large question mark over the science and thereby turning powerful gold into worthless straw. Equally important, he feared that by conceding the validity of the revisionist evidence one also accepted that the transmission belt between the capitalist present and the socialist future had been effectively cut. This anxiety can be seen in his response to Bernstein's claim that the number of wealthy people was increasing:

> If that were true then the date of our victory would not only
> be very long postponed, but we should never attain our goal.
> If it be capitalists who increase and not those with no
> possessions, then we are going even further from our goal
> the more evolution progresses, then capitalism grows stronger,
> not socialism.[23]

Kautsky's rather lacklustre counter-attack is, therefore, mainly a marshalling of alternative statistics supporting the contention that services are running normally and in accord with the historic timetable of class struggle. With Rosa Luxemburg, however, we witness a different tack. Although supportive of Kautsky in the revisionist controversy – and generally supportive for quite some years to come – a difference of approach can be detected. The revisionist evidence is not subject to a blanket dismissal: rather it is seen as a reflection of the historical development of capitalism, a development which Marxists must be cognizant of. This is seen as asserting the spirit of Marxism against the historically redundant letter of specific statements of

Marx and Engels. It is, of course, not seen as involving the adoption of the political stance of the revisionists. Bernstein's theoretical inadequacy, it is argued, prevents him from comprehending the true nature of the evidence he presents – and underlying this is a denial of the communist goal. Luxemburg is fully aware that Bernstein's ascription of 'utopianism' to Marx masks a substitution, not a rejection, of goals: 'His theory tends to counsel the renunciation of the social transformation, the final goal of Social Democracy, and inversely, to make social reforms, which are the means of the class struggle, into its end'.[24] In contrast, Luxemburg time and again asserts the absolute centrality of the socialist goal (i.e. communist society) to Marxism, for 'the final goal of socialism is the only decisive factor distinguishing the Social Democratic movement from bourgeois democracy and from bourgeois radicalism'.[25] Goals are so important because capitalism's inevitable collapse *could* produce barbarism rather than socialism. She refuses, however, to spell out the details of the socialist goal – a refusal which has its roots in both her overall conception of political and social struggle and in the scientistic 'anti-utopianism' of the Second International.

Luxemburg held a profound belief in the creativity of the proletariat, in its capacity to bring about future society in the course of its struggle with the bourgeoisie. It was a foolish political party, as she warned Lenin, which thought it could usefully impose its own *telos* on the broad movement. Such ultra-centralist utopianism would inevitably fall behind the actual achievements of the proletariat and would rapidly lose touch: 'revolutions', she argued, 'allow no one to play school master to them'[26] and even 'errors made by a truly revolutionary labour movement are historically infinitely more fruitful and more valuable than the infallibility of the best of all possible "central committees" '.[27] This should be seen as a restatement of Marx's own belief that the party should be a democratic institution where scientific insight and the lived experience of the proletariat co-mingle. There is, however, in Luxemburg a far greater reluctance than there is in Marx and Engels to speculate on future times – a product not only of Luxemburg's emphasis on proletarian creativity and spontaneity, but also of the absolute horror the charge of 'utopianism' held for Marxists of the Second International. In the strange new world of imperialism Luxemburg recognized the vital importance of goals, but, as with Kautsky and Bernstein, the need for goals jostles uneasily with the rejection of 'utopia'.

In Luxemburg's revealing letters to her 'comrade and lover', Leo Jogiches, the injury done to this imaginative and passionate woman by the narrow politics of the Second International is plain to see. She felt keenly the divide between what was deemed 'politics' and what 'personal life', as can be seen in a letter of 1894 on the issue of the Polish revolutionary journal, *The Workers' Cause*:

> Your letters contain nothing, but nothing except for *The Workers' Cause* . . . I want you to write me about your personal life. But not a single word! . . .What I can't stand is that wherever I turn, there's only one thing – 'The Cause.' It's boring, draining.[28]

The science/utopia distinction thus reproduced itself in a whole variety of other damaging dualisms. In moments of despair, Luxemburg was driven to conceive of happiness in terms of a rejection of politics:

> I cursed the damn 'politics' that stopped me from answering father's and mother's letters for weeks on end. I never had time for them because of those world-shaking problems . . . And my hate turned against you because you chained me to the accursed politics . . . Yesterday I was almost ready to give up, once and for all, the goddam politics (or rather the bloody parody of our 'political' life) and let the whole world go to hell. Politics is inane Baal worship, driving people – victims of their obsession, of mental rabies – to sacrifice their entire existence.[29]

Part of this is clearly the inevitable degree of hardship and sweat associated with any conceivable form of political activity – but it is also testimony to the deep psychic wounds inflicted on many militants by the constrained, positivist politics of the Second International. The whole atmosphere is revealed on the issue of women's rights. Karen Hunt, in a study of the British SDF (Social Democratic Federation), has shown how the 'Woman Question', although nominally supported (as an issue to be resolved after the revolution!), was in fact marginalized as, at best, merely a matter of personal conscience and, at worst, a dangerous diversion from the class struggle. Furthermore, it was seen by at least one contributor to *Justice* as a sign of women's immaturity that they could best be attracted to socialism by emphasis on enticing visions of the future: 'We ought to dazzle them with the wondrous transformation which will happen around us' and thereby 'captivate and charm the women with the beauties and possibilities of socialism'.[30] The priority supposed to be given to the restricted range of here and now issues, with merely a nod towards an abstractly conceived final goal, necessarily fragmented the broader perspective of a person like Luxemburg. Hence, despite her own spirited support for women's liberation and heroic attempts to blend the personal and political, the cruel choice she sometimes felt had to be made between life and politics.

All three thinkers lacked a vocabulary of anticipation. The terms 'utopia', 'utopian' and 'utopianism' are principally employed in a pejorative sense. They used them as synonyms for 'impossible', as in Luxemburg's: 'Either revisionism is correct concerning the course of capitalist development, and therefore the socialist transformation of society becomes a utopia. Or socialism is not a utopia; and therefore the theory of the "means of adaptation" is false'.[31] Sometimes the word 'utopia' meant, to quote Kautsky: 'an ideal picture of a perfect society',[32] a society which is very rigid and fixed and which is based upon naive assumptions about ease of implementation. On other occasions the term connoted unrealistic assumptions, so that, for Bernstein: 'one has not overcome Utopianism if one assumes that there is in the present, what is to be in the future'.[33] They also use the word as an historical category, deploying the category 'utopian socialism' according to the usage of the *Manifesto* and *Socialism: Utopian and Scientific*. All display sensitivity and sympathy to various utopian predecessors of Marx: Kautsky produced his *Thomas More and His Utopia*, in which the immense foresight of More is praised; Bernstein wrote a pioneering work on the radical political thought of the English Civil War,[34] and Luxemburg displayed a genuine respect for the ideas of Charles Fourier. None the less, they are at pains to distinguish clearly these pre-Marxian sages from authentic 'scientific socialism'. The three refuse to employ the language of the utopians, with its mixture of bold and subdued colours, broad and delicate brushstrokes. Their tragedy was that they had to speak of the future but, given their inhibitions about such speculation, lacked the means of articulation. Kautsky might praise More but he could never emulate him.

PLEKHANOV, KUSKOVA AND LENIN

The condition of Russia in the latter half of the nineteenth century – the co-existence of capitalist and pre-capitalist relations; a vast peasantry and comparatively small proletariat; a weak bourgeoisie and an autocratic state – clearly presented indigenous Marxists with the massive problem of applying the west European constructions of Marx and Engels in a very different environment. The career of Georgi Plekhanov, the founder of Russian Marxism, illustrates this problem. Plekhanov spent his early political life as a Narodnik, a member of a movement focusing on the supposed socialist tendencies of Russia's tens of millions of peasants. In particular, the Narodniks believed that Russia could skip the capitalist stage undergone in western Europe by building socialism on the communal basis of the peasant village community. Marx himself had toyed with this 'exceptionalist' theory in an ambiguous letter to Vera Zasulich in 1881 ('in order that [the village community] might function in this way one would first have to eliminate the destructive influences which assail it from every quarter and then to ensure the conditions normal for spontaneous development'); he continued in this vein with Engels in a Preface to the 1882 Russian edition of *The Manifesto*.[35] Plekhanov eventually rejected this theory and argued instead that Marx had uncovered universal laws of human history which all societies were subject to and that therefore Russia had to undergo a bourgeois revolution before it could pass through a socialist one. He used the category of 'utopian' to help theorize all this. Since 'being determines consciousness', Russia's backward conditions had generated backward theory. His previous Narodnism was now condemned as 'utopian socialism' and he saw himself as repeating, in the context of a time lag, Marx's championing of scientific socialism against its utopian predecessors.

Sufficiently aware of Marx and Engels' historical treatment of the emergence of utopian socialism, Plekhanov avoids blanket condemnation. Utopian socialism was once fresh and valuable in the conditions of early nineteenth-century western Europe but is now stale and reactionary in the context of late nineteenth-century Russia:

> Thus do utopian ideas journey from west to east, everywhere appearing as the heralds of the victory of that same capitalism against which they are revolting and struggling. But the

further they penetrate into the east the more their
historical significance changes. The French Utopians were in
their day bold innovators of genius; the Germans proved
much lower than they: and the Russians are now capable
only of frightening Western people by their antediluvian
appearance.[36]

Common to all, however, Plekhanov asserts, is a concern with
arbitrary ideals and an ignorance of the actual nature of society.
He was acutely aware of how economic forces were destroying
the 'ideal' of the village community and of the naivety of the old
strategies of terror, peasant jacqueries, etc. and yet equally
aware of their continuing attractiveness as ideological rivals to
Marxism. He thus one-sidedly stressed the objective moment of
society and played down the subjective moment. Future
speculation is seen as the mark of unreality and his irritation
with such speculation breaks out time and again in his portrayal
of a history moving majestically in the direction ordained by its
inherent laws:

Thus . . . we know nothing more hopeless than the
views of the Utopians of the end of the nineteenth century
. . . Each of them has his ready-made plan for saving the
Russian village commune and with it the peasantry generally:
each of them has his 'formula of progress'. But alas, life
moves on, without paying attention to their formulae, which
have nothing left but to find their own path, also
independently of real life, into the sphere of abstractions,
fantasies and logical mischances.[37]

Unfortunately, as he implicitly recognizes elsewhere, the
image of objective historical progress is particularly inappropriate
to Russian conditions. How is the bourgeois revolution supposed
to occur with a weak, vacillating bourgeoisie? What is to be the
relationship between the bourgeoisie, the peasants and the
proletariat, when all appear to want different things? The
recognition of such questions and the need for solutions led
Plekhanov to adopt a vanguardist strategy and its accompanying
concern with goals. Drawing on both internal Narodnik and
external Social Democratic sources, he called on the socialist
intelligentsia 'to provide the working class with the possibility to
take an active and fruitful part in the future political life of
Russia',[38] by means of political enlightenment. The newly-

enlightened working class would then provide the bourgeoisie
with both backbone and muscle to achieve the bourgeois
revolution and thereby create the conditions for the eventual
socialist revolution. Not surprisingly, in the various manifestos
he produced, Plekhanov had to spell out in some detail the
anticipated course of future events, if only to explain to the
proletariat why they should help their class enemies seize
power! He takes pains, however, to deny that there is anything
utopian in all this, to stress that he is not 'falling into utopian
fantasies about the social and international organization of the
future'.[39] He is, in fact, quite unable to marry convincingly at the
theoretical level that part of his theory which rejects future
speculation in favour of the objective movement of things and
that which recognizes the practical complexities of Russian
society and the consequent need, grudgingly conceded, for
goals and alternatives. All we get are contradictory statements
such as (with reference to the 'laws of history') that one must
have 'the ability to submit to those laws, that is, incidentally, to
combine them in the most favourable manner',[40] or vague
metaphors such as Marx's 'shortening and lessening the birth-
pangs' of socialism.

The dangers of leaving the historical process to its own
devices were forcibly brought home by the appearance on the
scene of revisionism and economism. Although Bernstein's
claim that a majority of Russian Social Democrats were close to
his own position was a hollow boast, there was an undoubted
revisionist tendency in Russia at the end of the nineteenth
century. The classic document of Russian revisionism is the
Credo of E. D. Kuskova. As with Bernstein, the tone of the
approach is 'realistic'. Classes are motivated by the self-
interested pursuit of accessible goals: 'The fundamental law that
can be discerned from studying the workers' movement is that
of the line of least resistance'.[41] In the west, where the political
struggle has been uppermost, the working class has almost
never won democratic rights for itself. This has been the task of
the bourgeoisie; the workers merely use what they have been
given. Bernsteinism is merely the inevitable stance of a working
class that has accommodated itself in the new environment. The
socialist party's scaled-down goals reflect the new reality:

The party will recognise society: its narrow corporative and,
in the majority of cases, sectarian tasks will broaden into

social tasks and its striving to seize power will be transformed into a desire for change, for the reform of contemporary society along democratic lines that are adapted to the present state of affairs, with the object of protecting, in the most complete and effective way, (all) the rights of the labouring classes. The concept of politics will be expanded, acquiring a truly social meaning, and the practical demands of the moment will acquire greater weight and will be able to count on receiving greater attention than has hitherto been the case.[42]

In Russia, however, the conditions are different. The political struggle is too difficult a road for the working class. The way forward is the economic struggle. This is the only realistic way in which the workers can improve their conditions and is the path socialists should promote. The political task of the socialists is to support the liberal bourgeoisie in their attempt to gain basic political rights. An autonomous workers' political party is out of the question:

> Talk of an independent workers' political party is nothing but the result of transplanting alien aims and alien achievements on to our soil . . . For the Russian Marxist there is only one way out: participation in, i.e. assistance for, the economic struggle of the proletariat and participation in liberal opposition activity.[43]

'Economism', a doctrine its opponents tended to lump together with revisionism, also stressed the immediate goals of the working class. The pace and direction of the struggle was to be determined by the workers themselves and not by an external socialist intelligentsia. As a representative of this trend, K. M. Taktarev, put it:

> This struggle . . . must be waged by the actual workers' organisations so that these workers' political demands rest on what they themselves recognise as their general political requirements and current interests, so that these demands should be the demands of the workers' (guild) organisations, so that they are really worked out by them together and advanced by all these workers' organisations together, on their own individual initiative in accordance with the collective common will of their members.[44]

This whole strategy envisaged, not a creative proletariat boldly striding towards socialism à la Luxemburg, but rather a highly circumscribed day-to-day struggle over (principally) wages and conditions.

Such currents were a dagger at the throat of Plekhanov. They could be interpreted as implying that Russia was not moving in the law-guaranteed direction Plekhanov claimed and that his 'combining of historical laws' and 'shortening of birth-pangs' was, in effect, the imposition of external goals on the objective movement – utopianism, in short. Plekhanov was one of the first to launch into an attack on Bernstein and he did so with the vehemence of one who is fighting for the very life of his system. Unfortunately, much like Kautsky, he tended simply to reject Bernstein's evidence and assert the continuing validity of orthodoxy. Thus, for example, Bernstein's claim that the number of property owners was increasing was *a priori* wrong – if Bernstein was correct, Marxism would be disproved:

> all Marxists have been convinced that the growth of social wealth in capitalist society goes hand in hand with the growth of social inequality and a decline in the number of property-owners. Had Herr Bernstein been able to prove the reverse, it would have to be acknowledged that he had dealt Marxism a mortal blow. (And then, indeed, all talk of the social revolution would be useless.)[45]

Neither Bernstein nor Russian revisionism and economism could shake Plekhanov's faith in his 'scientific' theory of history.

A younger generation of Russian Marxists rallied to the cause of Plekhanov – amongst them Lenin. In articles and pamphlets Lenin defended 'orthodoxy' – most notably in *What is to be Done?* Like Luxemburg, however, his defence implicitly acknowledged part of the revisionist evidence. Revisionism and economism, by 'bowing to spontaneity' or, in other words, by moving in the direction and at the rate of the working class, were allowing that class to work itself into an historical cul-de-sac. In perhaps his most famous proposition, Lenin maintained that the working class on its own could only develop trade union and not true socialist consciousness – the latter emerges in the intelligentsia who have to bring it to the workers:

> It would have to be brought to them from without. The history of all countries shows that the working class,

exclusively by its own effort, is able to develop only trade union consciousness, i.e., the conviction that it is necessary to combine in unions, fight the employers, and strive to compel the government to pass necessary labour legislation, etc. The theory of socialism, however, grew out of the philosophic, historical and economic theories elaborated by educated representatives of the propertied classes, by intellectuals.[46]

Lenin, therefore, could only defend Plekhanov and 'orthodoxy' by emphasizing the conscious moment of Plekhanov's approach. History, unless firmly taken in hand, has no guaranteed *telos*.

In *What is to be Done?*, Lenin endorses the value of dreaming as a part of this conscious moment. He has just outlined what he sees as the way forward for the movement, and concludes: 'That is what we should dream of!' He then expresses the classic Second International knee-jerk reaction to future speculation: ' "We should dream!" I wrote those words and became alarmed'. This, however, is not the preface to a denunciation of dreaming, but to a piece of pure fantasy where he champions the cause of dreaming against the 'realistic' economists:

> I imagined myself sitting at a 'unity conference' and opposite me were the *Rabocheye Dyelo* editors and contributors. Comrade Martynov rises and, turning to me, says sternly: 'Permit me to ask you, has an autonomous editorial board the right to dream without first soliciting the opinion of the Party committees?' He is followed by Comrade Krichevsky, who . . . continues even more sternly: 'I go further, I ask, has a Marxist any right at all to dream, knowing that according to Marx mankind always sets itself the tasks it can solve and that tactics is a process of the growth of Party tasks which grow together with the Party!'

Lenin, after a further piece of mock drama, quotes extensively from the radical literary critic and philosopher D. I. Pisarev (1840–1868):

> The very thought of these stern questions sends a cold shiver down my spine and makes me wish for nothing but a place to hide in. I shall try to hide behind the back of Pisarev . . . 'There are rifts and rifts,' wrote Pisarev of the rift between dreams and reality. 'My dream may run ahead of the natural march of events or may fly off at a tangent in a direction in

which no natural march of events will ever proceed. In the
first case my dream will not cause any harm; it may even
support and augment the energy of the working man . . .
There is nothing in such dreams that would distort or
paralyse labour-power. On the contrary, if man were completely deprived of the ability to dream in this way, if he
could not from time to time run ahead and mentally conceive,
in an entire and complete picture, the product to which his
hands are only just beginning to lend shape, then I cannot at
all imagine what stimulus there would be to induce man to
undertake and complete extensive and strenuous work in the
sphere of art, science, and practical endeavour . . . The rift
between dreams and reality causes no harm if only the
person dreaming believes seriously in his own dream, if he
attentively observes life, compares his observations with the
castles in the air, and if, generally speaking, he works
conscientiously for the achievement of his fantasies. If there
is some connection between dreams and life then all is well.

In his conclusion Lenin explicitly pits this positive assessment of
dreaming against revisionist and economistic 'realism': 'of this
kind of dreaming there is unfortunately too little in our
movement. And the people most responsible for this are those
who boast of their sober views, their "closeness" to the
"concrete" . . .'.[47] That this defence is not a solitary, youthful
caprice is shown by its reiteration in 1915. In private jottings of
that year (published after his death as *Conspectus of Aristotle's
Metaphysics*), in the course of a discussion of the role of fantasy
in idealist thought, Lenin both asserts the value of fantasy in
science and shows the continuing influence Pisarev's passage
has had on him: 'it would be stupid to deny the role of fantasy,
even in the strictest science: cf. Pisarev on useful dreaming, as
an impulse *to* work, and on empty day-dreaming'.[48] For Lenin,
therefore, fantasy was in Marxism as of right.

An interesting link between Pisarev and Lenin is their
admiration for the revolutionary writer Nikolai Chernyshevsky
(1828–1889). Pisarev, according to Chernyshevsky's biographer,
'claimed to be his pupil'[49] in developing the idea of a didactic
use of form (i.e. the need to harness modes of expression to the
goal of fundamental individual and social change). Pisarev's
advocacy of dreaming can be seen as a part of this development.
Lenin's admiration is well known, as is his most concrete

expression of it in naming his 1902 work after Chernyshevsky's novel, *What is to be Done?* (1863). This remarkable novel, which influenced a generation of Russian revolutionaries, is primarily a piece of socialist and feminist utopianism. The central character, Vera Pavlovna, creates an advanced co-operative workshop, reminiscent of the work of Robert Owen (who was an important influence on Chernyshevsky) and, in a series of dreams, has visions of a better world which bear the distinct hallmark of Charles Fourier. Throughout, Chernyshevsky stressed the feasibility of the various goals portrayed – that in times past 'men . . . caught glimpses of these thoughts when they were but marvellous and ravishing utopias; now it has been demonstrated that they can be realized . . . that these thoughts are good, with nothing of the marvellous about them'.[50] Lenin's relationship to Chernyshevsky bears some resemblance to that between Marx and Engels on the one hand and Saint-Simon, Owen and Fourier on the other. Chernyshevsky was, for Lenin, a 'Utopian Socialist' – one 'who dreamed of a transition to socialism through the old, semi-feudal peasant village commune' and who 'owing to the backwardness of Russian life, was unable to rise to the level of the dialectical materialism of Marx and Engels'.[51] However, like Marx and Engels with their utopian predecessors, he is unable to conceal the enthusiasm he feels for his. Thus 'our great Russian utopian', that 'genius', is commended – not just for his critique of Tsarist society, but also for his 'brilliant predictions' concerning the development of Russia and his rejection of inflexible, dogmatic politics. Writing in 1920, Lenin employed an aphorism of Chernyshevsky's, not for the first time, against dogmatism:

> Our theory is not a dogma, but a *guide to action*, said Marx and Engels. The greatest blunder, the greatest crime, committed by such 'out-and-out' Marxists as Karl Kautsky, Otto Bauer, etc., is that they have not understood this and have been unable to apply it at crucial moments of the proletarian revolution. 'Political activity is not like the pavement of Nevsky Prospekt' (the well-kept, broad and level pavement of the perfectly straight principal thoroughfare of St. Petersburg), N. G. Chernyshevsky, the great Russian socialist of the pre-marxist period used to say.[52]

It is surely no coincidence, therefore, that Lenin's most explicit defence of dreaming bears the title of Chernyshevsky's utopian novel.

In *The State and Revolution*, written between the February and October revolutions in 1917, Lenin brought his own dreaming power to bear on the nature of a socialist society. In a number of striking passages he departs from his exegesis of Marx and Engels' views and speculates on the nature of post-revolutionary society. The argument that this wasn't really future-gazing, because the revolutionary situation in Russia both demanded and suggested new structures, falls because Lenin deals with the higher as well as the lower phases of socialism/communism. There is, of course, the standard denunciation of utopianism, but by this is meant totally arbitrary and abstract speculation, hence:

> There is no trace of utopianism in Marx, in the sense that he made up or invented a 'new' society. No, he studied the birth of the new society out of the old, and the forms of transition from the latter to the former, as a natural-historical process.[53]

This is clearly the meaning Lenin attributes to the word 'utopia' in a discussion of the concept in 1912: 'In politics utopia is a wish that can never come true – neither now nor afterwards, a wish that is not based on social forces and not supported by the growth and development of political, class forces'[54] and it is in this sense that he makes the claim in the same discussion that 'Marxists . . . are hostile to all and every utopia'.[55] This is quite obviously not a denunciation of future speculation *per se*. The speculation in *The State and Revolution* was seen as the provision of that scientific goal without which the proletariat would lack direction. Thought on the outline of future society was, therefore, a necessary response to 'a most urgent problem of the day, the problem of explaining to the masses what they will have to do before long to free themselves from capitalist tyranny'.[56]

The clear dangers of this vanguardist approach were inevitably increased by Lenin's organizational novelties. Conceived as a response to the conditions of autocracy, the tightly centralized party always contained the potential for its own autocratic utopianism. The initial success, but continued isolation, of the Bolshevik revolution generated and legitimated the lifeless 'party line' of Stalinism, with its rhetorical long-term goals, opportunistic short-term strategies and tactics, and catch-all usage of the label 'utopian' against challenges to its 'scientific' pretensions.

CONCLUSION

The two giants of social democracy and communism emerged from this period – both claiming a bogus objectivity. Social democracy takes its stand on 'realism' and parliamentary democracy, condemning as 'utopian' anything which over-shoots its own little idyll of liberal-democratic capitalism. Communism, on the other hand, offers 'scientific leadership' and sterile party goals. They are the fitting progeny of the 'scientific' fear of the future which could not do without the future; of that low-grade 'non-utopian' utopianism, so prevalent in the Second International. Yet, as we saw, not all was gloom. In particular, Lenin's defence of dreaming and Luxemburg's emphasis on the creativity of ordinary people point to a much fuller conception of Marxism. Also, as we shall see in the next chapter, the Second International period witnessed a number of very distinctive theoretical contributions which bear directly on the issue of utopianism.

CHAPTER 4

GOLDEN AGES AND MYTHS

GOLDEN AGES

One way to give greater substance and plausibility to an image of the future is to show that such arrangements once obtained in the past. The use of golden history has itself a venerable and varied history. Plato used the example of ancient humanity in the *Laws*, to show that truly moral societies have existed on the earth. In medieval times, the period before the Fall became the new lost paradise and could, for a John Ball, prompt the famous question: 'Whan Adam dalf and Eve span, wo was thanne a gentilman?' The theory of the 'Norman yoke,' popular in seventeenth-century radicalism, portrayed a free, equal and democratic Anglo-Saxon society which was destroyed by the tyrannical Normans. Amongst modern political thinkers, Rousseau looks back to Sparta in his *Discourse on the Sciences and Arts*; whilst Hegel extols the virtues of ancient Athens in *The Philosophy of History* and the *Phenomenology of Spirit*. These snapshots of bliss have fulfilled a whole range of functions: some have used them as components in a theory of historical decline, where the lost paradise was an irretrievable pinnacle; others consign them to the happy childhood of humanity, an initial phase which had to give way to a more prosaic maturity, whilst others advocate a return to the pristine purity of the old days; a process involving a rejection of all the accretions of succeeding centuries. The response we are interested in is the use of these memories of time past as both models of, and evidence for, a new Eden. This is not a call to return to the past but rather to incorporate the essential qualities of those times in the context, and on the basis, of modern conditions – renaissance, not regression.

That much of this is bad history, made up of mythic, poetic and religious aspects and reflecting both wish-fulfilment and the elementary nature of historical knowledge in these times, should not obscure the methodological intent of those who appealed to it. They considered themselves to be dealing with real historical events, to be distinguished from rhetorical resort to fable or from the construction of abstract states of nature as explanatory devices. It was the *reality* of these wonderful events which made the whole enterprise worthwhile, for if ancestors once sustained, for example, a more flexible division of labour, held goods in common and practised direct democracy, such arrangements are obviously humanly possible and the old could serve as a reliable guide for the new. But the glamour of that which was past, and therefore 'real', allowed one to be both scientific and utopian. It was possible to speculate about the future by talking about the past. Discussion of an ancient freedom could become the arena for anticipation of future freedom. Thus, in an age of scientific Marxism, the safe scientific past could become a focus for suspect utopian longings and fantasies.

Marx penned some very negative sentiments against a certain type of revivalism in *The Eighteenth Brumaire of Louis Bonaparte.* His target was the co-option by revolutionaries of the imagery of their predecessors; the apparently paradoxical fact that the challenge of the new generates a retreat into the past, that:

> just when they seem engaged in revolutionising them-
> selves and things, in creating something that has never yet
> existed, precisely in such periods of revolutionary crisis they
> anxiously conjure up the spirits of the past to their service
> and borrow from them names, battle cries and costumes.[1]

He does distinguish between the partially creative use of the past by the great bourgeois revolutionaries, Cromwell, Danton, Napoleon etc., where revivalism could act as a stimulant, and its conservative and purely rhetorical use by the French revolutionaries of 1848–51. In the case of the former:

> the awakening of the dead . . . served the purpose of
> glorifying the new struggles, not of parodying the old; of
> magnifying the given task in imagination, not of fleeing from
> its solution in reality; of finding once more the spirit of
> revolution, not of making its ghost walk about again.[2]

Nevertheless, even this illustrious usage contained a large measure of self-deception, a necessary element of mystification with respect to goals and motives. They found in antique 'ideals and . . . art forms, the self-deceptions they needed in order to conceal from themselves the bourgeois limitations of the content of their struggle'.[3] Modern revolutionaries, by contrast, must orientate themselves to the future and not allow the memory of past glories to seduce them away from pressing tasks. 'The social revolution of the nineteenth century cannot draw its poetry from the past, but only from the future.'[4] Having noted this, however, not too much should be built upon it. Marx is concerned here with the *self-delusory* use of historical *imagery* and cannot be interpreted as ruling out a scientific and revolutionary appropriation of the past. However, bearing in mind Engels' later enthusiasm for ancient Germanic society, we might note Marx's methodological fears of 1844 on this topic. The *Contribution to the Critique of Hegel's Philosophy of Law* expresses Marx's worry about both the specificity of ancient forms and the temptation to read present conditions back into the past. He thus takes to task those 'Germanomaniacs' who

> seek our history of freedom beyond our history in the
> primeval Teutonic forests. But what difference is there
> between the history of our freedom and the history of the
> boar's freedom if it can be found only in the forests? Besides,
> it is common knowledge that the forest echoes back what you
> shout into it. So let us leave the ancient Teutonic forests in
> peace![5]

In Engels' *The Origin of the Family, Private Property and the State* we can observe both sensitivity towards and admiration for earlier social formations. The similarities between Engels' portrait of ancient society and the classic Marxist vision of communism are obvious. It is hard to avoid the conclusion that one of the principal purposes of the work was to show the feasibility of free institutions and the transient nature of capitalism. The whole piece, in fact, was conceived as a means of getting socialist propaganda past the German Anti-Socialist Law by disguising it as a 'neutral' scientific treatise. The work's subtitle is 'In the light of the researches of Lewis H. Morgan' and it draws heavily on the anthropological data of this American writer (particularly his work on the Iroquois). As the Preface to *The Origin* makes clear, Marx himself, if he had lived, had planned to publish on Morgan's findings, and Engels claimed that 'the following chapters constitute, in a sense the fulfilment of a bequest'.[6] Morgan, Engels declared, had independently rediscovered the materialist conception of history and provided crucial evidence for humanity's first stage. Engels lovingly describes the time when there was no bourgeois family, no state and no private property – a time when liberty, equality and fraternity were manifest:

> Everything runs smoothly without soldiers, gendarmes or police; without nobles, kings, governors, prefects or judges; without prisons; without trials. All quarrels and disputes are settled by the whole body of those concerned. Although there are many more affairs in common than at present – the household is run in common and communistically by a number of families, the land is tribal property, only the small gardens being temporarily assigned to the households – still, not a bit of our extensive and complicated machinery of administration is required. There can be no poor and needy – the communistic household and the gens know their obligations towards the aged, the sick and those disabled in war. All are free and equal – including the women. There is as yet no room for slaves, nor, as a rule, for the subjection of alien tribes . . . This is what mankind and human society were like before class divisions arose.[7]

He also wants to show that this society was doomed, that it carried within itself the seeds of its own destruction – in short, that capitalism was a necessary, if unpleasant, development. Engels is thus aware of the darker side of ancient society, including its tribalism, undeveloped production and limited horizons. However, the work ends, most significantly, with a quote from Lewis Morgan in which, speculating on a better future society, he states: 'It will be a revival, in a higher form, of the liberty, equality and fraternity of the ancient gentes'.[8] Engels does appear to be suggesting in the use of this quote that communism will be the old order raised to a new level (in a letter of this period he had enthused: 'Morgan . . . concludes with directly communist propositions in relation to present-day society').[9] This use of revivalism by Engels is of a very specific type. It is not that he has come across a society which has so impressed him that he thinks future society must incorporate its essential features. Rather it is that he already has a vision of future society drawn from other sources and is merely casting around for evidence for its viability. It will not come as a surprise that one of the other sources which haunts Engels' book is Fourier. As he said in a letter to Karl Kautsky describing his purposes in *The Origin*: 'I must show how Fourier's genius anticipated Morgan in very many things'.[10] And although Engels refers to Fourier's *critique* of capitalism in this context, one cannot help feel the influence of Fourier (and the other two great utopian socialists) in the picture of ancient free society.

A number of years prior to Engels' work, Marx's son-in-law Paul Lafargue (1842–1911), in his exuberant *The Right To Be Lazy*, had used historical and anthropological data to raise the promise of a communism in which the lost natural individual would live again. History, for Lafargue, provided numerous examples of ennobling indolence, as, for example, in the leisured classes of ancient Greece and Rome and the holidays of the middle ages where there was 'leisure to taste the joys of the earth, to make love and to frolic, to banquet joyously in honor of the jovial god of idleness'.[11] In a passage reminiscent of both Fourier and Saint-Simon, he spells out the task of the proletariat:

> It must return to its natural instincts, it must proclaim the Rights of Laziness, a thousand times more noble and more sacred than the anaemic Rights of Man concocted by the metaphysical lawyers of the bourgeois revolution. It must accustom itself to working but three hours a day, reserving the rest of the day and night for leisure and feasting.[12]

Unlike the ancient and medieval world, where the natural was based on exploitative social relations and low technology, the future would combine equitable relationships with extensive mechanization. The publication of Engels' work reinforced this line of thought in Lafargue. Lafargue's letters reveal that he was familiar with Morgan and the literature on pre-history before Engels' book appeared (Engels said himself of *The Origin* that 'there are things in it just in his [i.e. Lafargue's] line').[13] However, in a letter of 1885, Lafargue told Engels, after reading the first few chapters of *The Origin*, that 'Your exposition has been a revelation to me'.[14] His own *The Evolution of Property from Savagery to Civilization* (1890), therefore, does seem to be following Engels (though curiously he is only briefly mentioned once) in putting into the centre of the stage Morgan's positive account of primitive communism. The chapter on this topic is explicitly conceived as a polemic against those who argue for the historical ubiquity of capitalist relations – in particular against Huxley's dismissal of Rousseau's communist state of nature. Although, like Engels, he is aware of the necessary defects of this ancient form, it is clear the he conceives of the communism to come as embodying at a higher level the basic spirit of the earlier mode. He thinks, for example, that the modern individual is, by and large, both mentally and physically inferior to archaic humanity and will require the conditions of socialism to regain these standards:

> It will require an education beginning at the cradle and prolonged throughout life and continued for several genera-tions to restore to the human being of future society the vigour and perfection of the senses which characterise the savage and the barbarian.[15]

His conclusion is unambiguous: '[The] final communist and international revolution of property is inevitable; already, in the midst of bourgeois civilisation, do the institutions and com-munistic customs of primitive times revive'.[16] All these points are reiterated in his *La Propriété: Origine et Évolution* (1895), in which the debt to Engels is acknowledged. Engels himself read this work and in a letter to Lafargue, whilst criticizing some points of fact and presentation, he in no way attacks the idea of the 'return' of primitive communism.

The whole 'return' thesis is succinctly summarized in Bebel's immensely popular and pioneering book on Marxist feminism, *Die Frau und der Sozialismus*. This work in its first editions, sometimes for legal purposes retitled *Die Frau in der Vergangenheit, Gegenwart, und Zukunft* (Woman in the Past, Present, and Future), predated Engels' book and contained no reference to a 'return'. Later editions, however, show Engels' influence. Thus by the turn of the century, in the thirty-third edition, the leader of the German party could draw together the work of Morgan and Engels and the rest of the burgeoning material on primitive communism. Bebel, who was a self-taught, long-standing member of the workers' movement and had written a study of the life and teachings of Fourier, was, contrary to the impressions of both Masaryk and Bismarck, more willing to speculate about the future than most of his colleagues. Steinberg, in an examination of the social science and party literature sections of workers' libraries in Germany before 1914, has shown that

Bebel's book was far and away the most purchased and borrowed: 'A contemporary critic of social democracy had already found that Bebel's picture of the future state "had undoubtedly created a greater belief in socialism in the popular mind than Karl Marx's biting criticism of bourgeois economics was ever able to" '.[17] Bebel's ability to flesh out the goal of the historical process, conceived in terms of a 'return', fed the utopian appetites of a working class whose needs he appreciated. His chapter on woman in the future concludes on a clear 'return' note:

> Human society has traversed, in the course of thousands of years, all the various phases of development, to arrive in the end where it started from – communistic property and complete equality and fraternity . . . Nevertheless, while man returns to the starting point in his development, the return is effected upon an infinitely higher social plane than that from which he started . . . The 'Golden Age' that man has been dreaming of for thousands of years, and after which they have been longing, will have come at last.[18]

Bebel's adoption reveals the extent to which the 'return' thesis penetrated Marxist perspectives of that period.

Engels' portrayal of primitive communism has remained a stimulus to Marxists in this century. Two thinkers from the 1930s, Reich and Strachey, should suffice as examples. Reich, in *The Imposition of Sexual Morality*, a work which, he says, 'may be considered the direct continuation of the Morgan and Engels studies',[19] argues the case for an ancient, sexually free matriarchy and speculates that, in the future society: 'The original conditions of primitive communism return once more on a higher economic and cultural level as the sex-economic management of sexual relationships'.[20] Strachey's *The Theory and Practice of Socialism*, in a significantly entitled chapter, 'Origin and Future of the State', concludes an Engelsian account of human history with this observation on the future citizens of communism:

> The idea of refusing to play their part, to the best of their ability, in the social and productive life of the community will no more occur to those citizens of the future than the idea of refusing to dig, to hunt or to come to the general assembly of the tribe occurred to an Iroquois or a pre-Homeric Achaean gentile.[21]

A utopian concern with the past can be seen in the work of two thinkers from Britain and Ireland. William Morris (1834–96) and James Connolly (1868–1916), each in his highly distinctive way, turned to history as part of their future orientation.

A strong claim could be made that Morris was the first self-consciously utopian Marxist. Although he did not describe himself as utopian his work not only abounds with visions of the future but also seeks to justify the revolutionary function of such anticipation. The titles of some of his lectures and articles convey this: 'How We Live and How We Might Live', 'The Hopes of Civilization' and 'The Society of the Future', for example. He also, in *News From Nowhere*, produced a classic utopia. Such visions he argues, motivate: 'these dreams for the future, make many a man [*sic*] a Socialist whom sober reason deduced from science and political economy and the selection of the fittest would not move at all'.[22] They also provide direction:

> It is, then, no less than reasonable that those whom we try to involve in the great struggle for a better form of life than that which we now lead should call on us to give them at least some idea of what that life may be like.[23]

Throughout, a particular conception of the medieval world shaped important aspects of his vision of communism. Although he was fully aware of the many evils which accompanied feudal society, he also claimed that this society displayed qualities which capitalism had destroyed but which communism would revive. There is a link here with the Morgan/Engels thesis: in an article of 1890, Morris connects the vigorous creativity of the tribes which administered the *coup de grâce* to the Roman Empire to their comparative nearness to the old primitive communism. Long before this Engelsian detail was added, however, Morris, like his great mentor Ruskin, was under the spell of Victorian medievalism. In particular Morris saw in medieval craft labour an anticipation of what free labour in communism will be like. The medieval craftsperson experienced none of the divisions which fragment and degrade labour under capitalism: that between manual and intellectual labour, between 'great art' and mere manufacture; and between pleasure and work. This labour was also essentially co-operative (one should note in these respects Morris' admiration for the work of Owen and Fourier). Morris was fully aware of the ideological advantage to be gained in showing that free labour has existed historically: 'it is possible for man to rejoice in his work, for, strange as it may seem to us to-day, there have been times when he did rejoice in it'.[24] For Morris, not only is such labour the paradigm for human activity, but its products represent the pinnacle of human achievement to date. It is in this double sense that Morris argued, in 1889: 'In the future, therefore, our style of architecture must be Gothic Architecture'.[25] Throughout his description of communist England in *News From Nowhere*, one of the highest compliments he pays to objects is that they are, or resemble, 'fourteenth-century' artifacts – and the place seems to be positively saturated with such things. The post-medieval world is seen as shoddy and inhuman. The Renaissance ('the miseries of the New Birth')[26] is derided, its 'great men were really but the fruit of the blossoming-time, the Gothic period'.[27] Thomas More 'must be looked upon rather as the last of the old than the first of the new'.[28] And so on and so forth. The revolution which will usher in the new world is itself described in terms of the achievement of the ancient tribes: 'So shall we be our own Goths, and at whatever cost break up again the new tyrannous Empire of Capitalism'.[29]

Morris was conscious of the inevitable subjective element in his vision of communism – that his radicalized 'Merrie England-ism' would not be shared by all. In a review of Bellamy's *Looking Backward*, for example, he acknowledged the persuasive charm which the author's 'high-tech' utopia might exercise on many readers. Communism may be inevitable, but the details of its anticipation, as of its actuality, could not be authoritatively determined by one individual. As Morris wrote, in 1889: 'a man's vision of the future of society . . . must always be more or less personal to himself'.[30] This was not interpreted as a recipe for relativism – some visions were more objectively grounded than others – but rather as enjoining a pluralist approach whereby people themselves would decide which visions they found plausible and engage in the free and voluntaristic enterprise of creating socialism.

The Gothic revivalism associated with the names of Ruskin and Morris struck roots in the British labour movement at the end of the nineteenth and beginning of the twentieth century. Keir Hardie, who called Morris 'the greatest man whom the Socialist movement has yet claimed in this country',[31] could speak of Europe 'from the beginning of the thirteenth to the middle of the fifteenth century' as a period when 'there was neither Millionaires nor Paupers . . . but a rude abundance for all'.[32] David Howell, in his perceptive sutdy of the ILP,[33] has written of the power which images of 'The world we have lost' and rural arcadias had over members of this party. He argues that some of the support for the Boer cause amongst these people arose from the perception of the supposed 'innocence' of the Boers. In the phenomenon of Guild Socialism the further influence of Morris and Ruskin can be found, overlaid with syndicalist conceptions. In short, the imagery of 'Merrie England' exercised great fascination for many on the left and influenced their particular conceptions of future society.

James Connolly, in his attempt to combine Irish nationalism with Marxism, looked to a Gaelic past as an anticipatory model of the new Ireland. In 1897, in the Belfast journal *Shan Van Vocht* (edited by Alice Milligan), he spelled out what was to be a leitmotif of his work: 'Nationalism without Socialism – without a reorganization of society on the basis of a broader and more developed form of that common property which underlay the social structure of Ancient Erin – is only national recreancy'.[34] A major influence on Connolly was the Gaelic Revival in Ireland at the end of the nineteenth century. Institutions like the Gaelic Athletic Association (founded 1884), which sought to spread interest in 'native' Gaelic sports against 'alien' English pursuits, and The Gaelic League (founded 1893), with its goal of 'de-Anglicising Ireland' through the promotion of Irish language and culture, all stressed the integrity and contemporary validity of Gaelic traditions. Connolly was sympathetic to this revival but insisted that it move beyond genteel enthusiasm and become incorporated into the socialist transformation of Ireland. Another important influence was our old friend the anthropological literature on 'primitive society' and the work of Morgan in particular. In 'Erin's Hope . . . The End And The Means', Connolly noted that: 'Recent scientific research by such eminent sociologists as Letourneau, Lewis Morgan, Sir Henry Maine, and others has amply demonstrated the fact that common ownership of land formed the basis of primitive society in almost every country',[35] whilst in *Labour in Irish History* he enthused that Morgan's *Ancient Society* provided the 'key' which 'will yet unlock the doors which guard the secrets of our native Celtic civilisation'.[36] Engels' *The Origin* is nowhere mentioned, which casts some doubt on Greaves' claim in his biography of Connolly that 'probably he had read Unterman's translation of

Engels's *Origin of the Family*.[37] Familiarity with the concept of primitive communism would have been widespread in Marxist circles of the time – Marx himself had referred to its presence in ancient Celtic society as early as 1859, in his *Critique of Political Economy*. Ireland's achievement, according to Connolly, was that, unlike other societies, this egalitarian and democratic organization lasted well into historic times and was only destroyed by the English invaders with their individualistic and hierarchical ways. In Ireland, he argued, 'primitive communism . . . formed part of the well-defined social organization of a nation of scholars and students, recognized . . . as the inspiring principle of their collective life, and the basis of their national system of jurisprudence'[38] and he praises these 'Celtic forefathers, who foreshadowed in the democratic organization of the Irish clan the more perfect organization of the free society of the future'.[39]

A modern advocacy of Connolly's stance on Celtic Communism can be found in Peter Berresford Ellis' *A History of the Irish Working Class* (1972). This work recognizes the political impulse behind the venture into ancient history made both by Connolly and some of his critics. He argues that 'the conservative forces of the Irish independence movement wanted Eoin MacNeill, a Celtic scholar of wide repute, to academically destroy Connolly's theories on early Irish society'.[40] They clearly saw the radical implications of Connolly's perspective and wished to replace it with one which stressed inequality and private ownership in ancient Ireland. Ellis doggedly defends Connolly.

Modern scholarship has shown that there is much in these various 'golden ages' which is simplistic and mistaken. In the case of the 'primitive communism' of Morgan/Engels/Connolly, it has been demonstrated that such societies could simultaneously reject ultimate individual rights to property *and* countenance fundamental inequalities of use. As to Morris, it has been argued that he vastly overrated the centrality and spread of craft labour is what was in fact a thoroughly un-Merrie England. As Robert Blauner has put it: 'craftsmen, far from being typical workers of the past era, accounted for less than ten per cent of the medieval labour force, and the peasant, who was actually the representative labourer was . . . practically nothing more than a working beast'.[41] There is also the danger of falling into what philosophers have called the 'naturalistic fallacy', that is, of attempting to derive an 'ought' from an 'is' (or, in this case, from a 'was'). A 'good' past is derived from the value 'good' and not from the condition of being 'past'. The past, as such, is value-free and only gains modern significance by an act of modern evaluation. The fact of primitive communism cannot, in itself, imply the future desirability of communism. There are also clear dangers in projecting on to advanced societies characteristics which belong to less advanced forms – what was appropriate to medieval England may not be so in a highly developed socialist economy. It should also be noted that nineteenth- and early twentieth-century visions of the golden age often developed into particularly poisonous forms of right-wing utopianism – most notoriously of all in the Fascist cult of the Volk. This, however, is not the full story. The historical speculation of the various thinkers discussed was by no means all fantasy – they had locked into genuinely different, and instructive, societies. Also, such writers raise the question of the future by showing the mutable nature of past and present. They therefore strike at all ideological attempts to eternalize the present. Furthermore, they attempt to link the future to its past and thereby introduce an element of continuity into what might otherwise be arbitrary speculation. At the political level, the anchoring of socialism in national or other types of tradition is a powerful antidote to attempts to portray this ideology as somehow alien. There is also something powerfully attractive in golden ages, whether they be true or not, as can be seen in the continuing popularity of the fictionalized forms of fairy tales and legend. Whatever their other functions, they do seem to act as vehicles for a whole range of human aspirations. This raises the issue of the role of non-rational (as distinct from irrational) motivation, a topic to which the next section addresses itself.

MYTH

There has always been what one might term a rationalistic current in Marxism. It works with an Enlightenment model of the individual and its principal distinction is between knowledge and ignorance. This is its key to the central paradox of capitalism: that people put up with conditions not in their own interests. The ignorance which is false consciousness and alienation manifests itself in a variety of irrational beliefs and actions. However, once people break through this cocoon of illusion they will cease to behave in such a bizarre fashion. This is the spirit of Pottier's 'Internationale': 'Arise! ye starvelings from your slumbers/ Arise ye criminals of want/ For reason in revolt now thunders/ And at last ends the age of cant'. Such a view tends to privilege the bearers of knowledge: those who have emerged from the shadowy world of Plato's cave and have seen the light of the truth. There was a strong dose of this type of rationalism in much of the Marxism of the Second International and it helped fuel the obsession with science. Part of the reason, which itself was part of the problem, was that Marx and Engels failed to develop a psychology. They left a very poor legacy on the complexities of human motivation and most of their immediate successors felt little need to overcome this deficiency. A simple concept of the individual coexisted with simplistic socialist strategies.

A different perspective is to be found in the work of Georges Sorel (1847–1922). At first sight, Sorel's presence in this work might seem odd, for his articles and books contain strident denunciations of utopianism. In fact, he used the term 'utopianism' in a special fashion and in no way ruled out a future orientation. For Sorel, 'utopianism' was the abstract theorizing of intellectuals. In the nearest he ever got to outlining a golden age, he portrayed Homeric Greece as a society without a class of abstract intellectuals, in which a rich, concrete culture was spread throughout society; a society which was destroyed by the intellectualist culture of Socratic Greece. However, the revivalist use of golden ages is explicitly condemned by Sorel as a form of the 'utopianism' he is at pains to counter. In a specific reference to the Morgan/Engels thesis, he hoped that 'henceforth socialism will no longer depend on hypotheses about promiscuous Hawaiian tribes and other fine things of this kind'[42] and he expressed doubt about the supposed reasons for their advocacy:

> This is an advance that will not please certain French writers who are drawn perhaps as much to the promiscuity of primitive women as to the primitive communism of goods, and who indeed hope to see both of them reappear in future society.[43]

As this suggests, he thought that utopianism had got a foothold in Marxism. Both Marx and Engels, he argued, had succumbed at various times to grand historical schemata in which abstract societies rose and fell, culminating in the greatest abstraction of all: communism. Their orthodox followers had codified these into sterile formulae of which they were the authoritative guardians.

This is a part of Sorel's full-scale attack on the Enlightenment. He detests its mechanistic image of humanity and its naive political theory. An accurate account of the individual must take note of the intuitive, emotional and sexual aspects of the personality. It must also acknowledge that there are genuinely dark areas of the psyche: mysterious regions that cannot be explored with the puny instruments of rationalism. This in turn means that one cannot simplistically reduce behaviour to neat causal systems – the human being is an incredibly complex phenomenon and cannot be studied as if it were a piece of clockwork. A further consequence of this is that it undermines the notion of political theorist as social engineer, for individuals are not chess pieces to be guided by the omniscient intellectual. Instead, Sorel focuses on the complex behaviour of individuals and groups – what motivates them; how they have moved in history; the nature of their current relationships – with the aim of understanding their movements, as far as is possible, and providing support for progressive forces, but certainly not of 'controlling' them.

For Sorel, rationalistic intellectualism cannot understand reality. It cannot explain the actions of the self-sacrificing Napoleonic soldier, or of Giordano Bruno, who 'allowed himself to burn in Venice'.[44] 'Religions', says Sorel, 'constitute a particularly grave scandal for the intellectualist, for he can neither regard them as being without historical importance nor explain them'.[45] Underpinning this failure is a shallow model of the individual which totally omits the deep creative forces which are the well-springs of human existence. From this source come 'myths': epic images that express, and in turn reinforce, the mobilization of whole classes. The examples Sorel produces of this phenomenon include 'the myth of the Church militant' for Catholics, 'the return of Christ and the total ruination of the pagan world' for the early Christians, as well as the various epic aspirations generated in the French Revolution and in the drive for Italian unity. He also makes it clear that a future orientation is required in these myths:

> And yet we are not able to act without leaving the present, without thinking about that future which always seems

condemned to escape our reason. Experience proves that
some constructions of a future un-determined in time can
possess great effectiveness and have very few disadvantages
when they are of a certain nature; this occurs when it is a
question of myths in which the strongest inclinations of a
people, a party or a class are found, tendencies which present
themselves to the mind with the insistence of instincts in all
of life's circumstances, and which give an appearance of
complete reality to hopes of imminent action on which the
reform of the will is based.[46]

The fact that the resulting reality bears no relation to the original
anticipation is of no real consequence for Sorel. One can never
with any degree of accuracy predict what might occur. A myth is
meant to motivate – not predict – and its success is to be
measured in terms of the movement it generates:

Thus it matters little whether or not we know to what extent
myths contain those details that are actually destined to
appear on the plane of history in the future; myths are not
astrological almanacs; it is even possible that nothing contained in them will take place, as was the case with the
catastrophe expected by the first Christians.[47]

Sorel rejoices in the unfalsifiability of myth. Renan's criticism
that socialists are never discouraged by the failure of their
projects is said to miss the point – utopias can be proven false,
myths never. Myths should also never be broken down into
their component parts, for their power lies in their undifferen-
tiated wholeness.

The myth which is gripping the modern proletariat is the
myth of the general strike. At the time Sorel was developing his
theory of myth, he was involved with the French syndicalist
movement, and the notion of the autonomous group myth
neatly dovetails with the syndicalist belief that the working class
must emancipate itself, free from intellectual domination and
through its own experience of capitalism. The myth of the
general strike is comprised of the deepest feelings of opposition
to capitalism, including the urge to destroy it and replace it with
more equitable social relationships. It is, in Sorel's worlds:

the myth which encompasses all of socialism; that is to say,
an arrangement of images capable of evoking instinctively all
of the sentiments which correspond to the various manifes-

tations of the war waged by socialism against modern society. Strikes have inspired in the proletariat the noblest, deepest and most forceful sentiments that it possesses; the general strike groups them all into a general unified image and, by bringing them together, gives to each one of these sentiments its maximum intensity. Evoking very vivid memories of particular conflicts, it colours intensely all of the details of the composition presented to the mind. Thus we obtain that intuition of socialism that language could not give in a perfectly clear way – and we obtain it as an instantly perceivable whole.[48]

In this way the proletariat would move forward, not necessarily towards socialism (whatever that abstraction indicates), but forward as a powerful and integrated group. It is in this sense that he understands Bernstein's remark that the end is nothing and the movement everything.

This conception produces one major problem. If one is a syndicalist worker, then all one does is proceed to liberate oneself without intellectual leadership. If, on the other hand, one is a Leninist intellectual, one's role is also clear. Sorel, however, is an intellectual who both rejects intellectual leadership and stresses the proletarian character of revolution. He therefore rather paints himself out of the picture. Anything other than the rather nebulous conception of 'support' allows intellectualist utopianism in through the back door. What is required is an adaptation of Sorel's open-ended strategy which rejects both intellectual leadership *and* workerist definitions of progressive social forces. There is also danger in Sorel's theory of myth, for it is but a short step from the non-rational to the irrational. Sorel's own flirtation with fascism reinforces this point, as does his use by a number of later fascists, and his friends, the 'élitist' theorists Pareto and Michels, who developed similar ideas in a clearly fascist direction. At the end of the road lies Rosenberg's *Myth of the Twentieth Century*, where the 'philosopher' of the Third Reich grounds myth in 'the race' and employs it as an 'intellectual' fig leaf for anti-semitic ravings. This is only one development, however. Sorel's attack on shallow rationalism and his relatively sophisticated model of human motivation are of abiding interest and value. His rejection of reductionist accounts of 'irrational' behaviour points the way to a much broader conception of human aspiration.

CONCLUSION

The period of the Second International therefore saw a number of fascinating attempts to deal with the problem of the future. As with the thinkers in the previous chapter there was a powerful reluctance to use the word 'utopia' in any positive sense, and in so far as there was a greater openness to the future this was grounded in the supposedly solid structures of history and psychology. A common characteristic of the two approaches dealt with in this chapter is what one might term 'primitivism'. Both saw, in the so-called 'primitive' areas of either history or the mind, values and perspectives ignored by modern thought. In this respect they reflect a broad current of primitivism in the intellectual and artistic life of their time. The ultra-right, alas, proved to be much more competent at harnessing this powerful imagery. It was the National Socialists who managed to create a vision of a thousand-year *reich* out of romantic conceptions of Teutonic Knights, Saxon kings, and the mysterious promptings of 'the Blood'. The left all too often abandoned the field, muttering about reaction appealing to reaction. It was to take the radical appropriation of Freud to reintroduce into Marxism an awareness of the utopian potential of the 'primitive'.

CHAPTER 5

STALINISM AND AUTHORITARIAN UTOPIANISM

The Bolshevik Revolution ensured that Marxism achieved world significance in the form of Marxism-Leninism. This, of course, was not a foregone conclusion. 1917 was pregnant with possibilities – Stalinism was by no means inevitable. However, with the Stalinists' capture of the revolution in the 1930s, their newly minted Marxism-Leninism became inextricably linked with the fate of the Soviet Union. This had a number of deleterious consequences for Marxism:

1 The peculiar authoritarian utopianism entailed in this ideology became virtually hegemonic amongst the Marxist left throughout the world.
2 As the Soviet experience became itself a source of utopian inspiration, its failings were to generate disillusionment with Marxism itself.
3 The right was able plausibly to sell the equation totalitarianism = Stalinism = Marxism = utopianism.

1) The triumph of the Bolsheviks in 1917 immediately raised the issue of 'utopianism'. As we saw in chapter three, Kautsky saw the Bolshevik Revolution as 'utopian' in that it sought to build socialism on an inadequate base. This led to further 'utopianism', in Kautsky's view, because socialism, instead of being borne by the proletariat, as in the west, was in the Soviet Union grounded in the Bolshevik fraction. An inevitably simplistic and narrow party goal, and not society's own movement, was the motive force of the revolution. This in turn meant that the Bolsheviks had to use dictatorial methods to impose their vision against the actual dynamics of the society. This kind of conception was, for

Kautsky, pure utopianism – a throwback to what he considered to be the position of the utopian socialists:

> The idea that the only task of a socialist government is to put socialism into practice is not a Marxist, but a pre-Marxist, Utopian ideal. It represents socialism as an ideal picture of a perfect society. Like all ideal conceptions, its nature is very simple. Once it has been thought out, only the necessary power is required to realise this ideal everywhere and under all circumstances. When power does not produce this result immediately, it is due to treachery or cowardice. The only task of a socialist government is to put into practice the ideal conception of socialism. The more absolute its power, the sooner it will be able to do so.[1]

Thus, for a number of Marxists, the Bolshevik Revolution was itself a massive piece of unacceptable utopianism.

For Lenin, the revolution was a triumph of creative Marxism. 1917 had put the possibility of revolution on the historical agenda and the Bolsheviks had seized the moment. His theory of the 'weakest link' of capitalism legitimated the reversal of Marx's stricture that revolution would take place in the most developed capitalist society. The revolution in a backward society would lead to the collapse of the entire capitalist chain. Once this had occurred, the more advanced societies would help the less developed. October 1917 was the start of this process – the start of a new world. In this sense the revolution's existence owed much to the utopian spirit of Lenin: the creative dreaming, allied with analytical rigour, recommended in *What is to be done?*. His revolution did release great utopian energies. Two broad and potentially conflicting types of utopianism emerged. On the one hand there was an awareness of the dead weight of Tsarist Russia and of the consequent problem of carving a future out of such hard, resistant material. On the other there was a spirit of joyous optimism, a feeling that almost anything was possible: new cities, new culture, new people. In the heroic period the revolutionaries were gripped by both these impulses. As in France in 1789 and 1848, immense creative power was generated in all fields. The arts are a classic example. Futurists like Mayakovsky welcomed the revolution and threw themselves into the task of building what they saw as a totally new and exciting society. In the early stages they prospered, because their energies were of value to the Bolshevik strategy, particularly in the form of propaganda production. They were also fortunate in gaining the patronage of the highly civilized Minister for Enlightenment, Anatoly Lunacharsky. This was a golden summer for the many schools of art: Suprematists, Constructivists and the like. A poem of Mayakovsky captures the mood of the period:

> We will smash the old world
> wildly
> we will thunder
> a new myth over the world.
> We will trample the fence
> of time beneath our feet.
> We will make a musical scale
> of the rainbow.
>
> Roses and dreams
> debased by poets
> will unfold
> in a new light
> for the delight of our eyes
> the eyes of big children.
> We will invent new roses
> roses of capitals with petals of squares.[2]

In the area of personal and sexual relationships there was also great experimentation. Feminists like Alexandra Kollontai called for the surpassing of the bourgeois family and the various structures that had kept women enslaved under the old regime. The early legislation of the Bolshevik state went some way to enshrine progressive thought in these areas. In time, however, all this utopianism fell foul of the authoritarian utopianism of the Stalinist party. With the drift to Stalinism the party began to demand greater and greater conformity from artists, culminating in the very apotheosis of conformity: socialist realism. This was deemed to be the fixed role of art in the great plan. The traditional family also came to be seen as a useful tool in socialist construction and the old progressive legislation was removed.

Stalinism built upon a Leninist vanguard strategy which always had the potential for authoritarianism. In Stalinism, though lip-service was paid to the democratic form of the party, the principal justification for party rule was couched in terms of the scientific credentials of the party. Supposed scientific insight into the past, present and future permitted a disregard of the actual consciousness of the working class in many circumstances. The party was to have a 'leading role', thereby preventing the working class from spontaneously drifting into error. The *History of the Communist Party of the Soviet Union (Bolsheviks)* (1939) puts this gloss upon Lenin's attack on the Economists:

> Lenin showed that to extol the spontaneous process in the working-class movement, to deny that the Party had a leading role to play, to reduce its role to that of a recorder of events, meant to preach *khvostism* (following in the tail), to preach the conversion of the Party into a tail-piece of the spontaneous process, into a passive force of the movement, capable only of contemplating the spontaneous process and allowing events to take their own course . . . Lenin showed that . . . in reality the Socialist ideology arises not from the spontaneous movement, but from science. By denying the necessity of imparting a Socialist consciousness to the working class, the 'Economists' were clearing the way for bourgeois ideology.[3]

Since, according to this conception, science leads to one truth, society must be guided by one vision – the chain of 'reasoning' behind this is brought out in another place in the *History*:

> if the world is knowable and our knowledge of the laws of development of nature is authentic knowledge, having the validity of objective truth, it follows that social life, the development of society, is also knowable, and that the data of science regarding the laws of development of society are authentic data having the validity of objective truths.
>
> Hence the science of the history of society, despite all the complexity of the phenomena of social life, can become as precise a science as, let us say, biology, and capable of making use of the laws of development of society for practical purposes.
>
> Hence the party of the proletariat should not guide itself in its practical activity by casual motives, but by the laws of development of society, and by practical deductions from these laws.
>
> Hence Socialism is converted from a dream of a better future for humanity into a science.[4]

It is but a short step to the proposition that one person's access to science renders them an authoritative guide to future developments. The *History* was not willing publicly to go this far – but was willing to lay the foundations with its concepts of 'master theoretician':

> It may be said without fear of exaggeration that since the death of Engels the master theoretician Lenin, and after Lenin, Stalin and the other disciples of Lenin, have been the only Marxists who have advanced the Marxist theory and who have enriched it with new experience in the new conditions of the class struggle of the proletariat.[5]

By the end of the Second World War all remaining restraint disappeared. Stalin became the acknowledged authority on economics, history, philosophy, linguistics, music, etc. and on the overall direction of society – 'the great steersman of the masses'. Throughout, Stalin had brutally used his position in an attempt to drag the Soviet Union up to the level of the west. The international revolution had not been unleashed by the weakest link – one by one the European revolutions had collapsed. The imperative was now 'socialism in one country' – an impossibility for most Marxists, Marx included. It was, however, a conception that was more likely to strike a responsive key in the Soviet people than those that condemned the revolution to oblivion unless a highly improbable international revolution came to the rescue. Thus Trotsky's alternative of 'permanent revolution' carried within it a potentially insulting scenario of the 'advanced' west coming to the aid of the 'backward' Soviet Union. In Russia, in particular, 'socialism in one country' could easily dovetail into traditional Russian nationalism – a potent mixture, as Stalin found in the Second World War. The resulting vision was therefore a complex mixture in which long-term goals extracted from Marx/Engels/Lenin uneasily coexisted with highly rationalized short-term objectives. The genocidal meanderings which resulted were captured in a black joke of the period – 'Stalin's Marxism is a matter of trial and error – Stalin's errors, other people's trials'.[6]

In the midst of the terror, people dreamt of a better world. Wolfgang Leonhard, a school student in the Moscow of 1937, later recalled the hopeful fantasies draped around the figure of Marshal Blücher, the Commander-in-Chief of the Far Eastern Special Military District. At a time of mass arrests, the rumours maintained that Blücher's District was a veritable haven of legality. Leonhard remembers the following dialogue:

> 'There's no purge going on in the Far Eastern Military District.'
> 'No arrests at all?'
> 'Not quite that, of course, but only routine arrests, not what we're going through here.'
> 'But how can he do it?'
> 'Why shouldn't he? He has complete authority and he just doesn't let it happen. Ah, if only one could get to Vladivostok!' His eyes lit up at the thought.

The fantasy became richer – Blücher, it was said, had captured a whole trainful of security police sent to arrest him and had put all of them in prison. As Leonhard notes: 'At that time I assumed these rumours to be nothing but wishful thinking and today I am convinced of it. It was the last ray of hope in a hopeless situation'. Blücher, needless to say, was soon arrested and executed. Leonhard also reports that the idealistic youth were so gripped by the goal of building socialism that they were prepared to use the 'for the good of the cause' and 'one cannot make an omelette without breaking eggs' type of argument to justify the purges. Leonhard and his friends, who had lost parents and close friends to the terror, talked of historical necessity, of the primacy of the collective rather than the individual and of the inevitable loss of some good in the removal of the bad: 'We instinctively recoiled from the thought that what was happening in the mass arrests of these years was in diametrical opposition to our Socialist ideals'.[7]

The cretinization of the party involved in all this was duplicated on a world scale – the Moscow 'party line', no matter how dotty or dangerous, became, via the centralist institutions of the Third International, holy writ for the international communist movement. Every piece of politial lunacy (social democracy = social fascism), cynical *realpolitik* (the Nazi-Soviet pact), and theoretical nonsense (*Lysenko is Right* by James Fyfe)[8] was taken on board. For such 'dogmatic idealists', as Djilas termed them, no evidence was good against Stalinist Marxist-Leninism. Djilas used the expression about the Stalinist opponents of Yugoslavia's independent course in 1948. 'Communism, they insisted, never had been immune to error, but, being "scientific," it was self-correcting: loyalty to the final goal always had, always would, guarantee that mistakes would be corrected and the true path found again'.[9] Here was 'utopianism' in its very worst form!

2) For a whole generation of communist and radical intellectuals in the west, the Soviet Union fulfilled deep utopian longings. Here was a great experiment in social engineering, a new start – utopia had emerged from myth and was under construction. Time and again, as David Caute has shown, the image of the Soviet Union as 'the future' shines through the eulogies of western 'fellow-travellers': Steffens, 'the future is there';[10] Rolland, 'the hope, the last hope for the future of mankind';[11] O'Casey, 'Herald of a new life';[12] Gide, 'new Russia's Plans seem to me salvation'.[13] In all of this there was a complex mixture of realism, idealism, defensiveness, hope, mission, naivety and relativism. There were real achievements to praise and a willingness to see the best of things – also an often wilful blindness to the immense failings of the system. Many factors helped to produce this condition: the appalling economic disasters of the period (the Wall Street Crash, the general depression, mass unemployment, etc.) and the feebleness of social democracy, exemplified notably by Ramsay MacDonald's participation in the 'National' Government. There was a strong desire to protect the cause of socialism from the attacks of the capitalist establishment – and there was the reality of fascism: for if the choice was really between fascism and communism then one could not afford to be over-squeamish. The Spanish Civil War, in particular, forced many to think hard along these lines. Also the object of their desires, the 'utopia' itself, was always careful to put its best side forward – the Soviet Union took great pains to manage its image in the west. Furthermore, many of the friends of the USSR entertained the hope that sustained propaganda for the new society would help to accentuate all that was most positive. Some supporters, as Caute has ably demonstrated, preferred their utopia, at least in its present mode, to be abroad; for this was a Soviet experiment, the product of local conditions – not for export in its native form (hence the reluctance of these people to join their local communist parties). The revolution was a model which had to be adapted to the democratic traditions and more advanced base of the west. Some really rejected export completely: 'The fellow-travellers cultivated a convenient schizophrenia: they scorned democracy – at a distance; they invested their dreams of

positivistic experimentation and moral regeneration – at a distance'.[14] Others developed a type of primitivism, rejoicing in the hardness of the revolution; its supposed overcoming of the bourgeois values of individualism and the like. To those who spoke of 'the west in decline', here was a new heroic ethic – the astringent antidote to modern decadence. To intellectuals in revolt against their bourgeois backgrounds, such claims had an obvious appeal. Some, like Kim Philby, were prepared to accept total self-effacement, a life of dissimulation and dissemblance, as agents of the Soviet Union, agents of utopia. Whatever the other complex motivations behind Philby's decision, there were undoubted elements of both idealism and idealization – 'What Stalin does is Left',[15] he is reported to have said at this time. Looking back in 1968, whilst acknowledging a degree of disillusionment, he could still say defiantly: 'But, as I look over Moscow from my study window, I can see the solid foundations of the future I glimpsed at Cambridge'.[16]

A whole genre of devotional literature developed with titles such as Comrades and Citizens,[17] Red Virtue,[18] Dawn in Russia,[19] The Russia I Believe In,[20] Soviet Justice, and the Trial of Radek and Others.[21] In the same vein we might note the decision of the Webbs to produce a second edition (1937) of their 1935 work Soviet Communism: A New Civilization? – without the question mark![22] Much of this material certainly reads like a classic utopia. Two volumes can be taken as examples: Pat Sloan, Soviet Democracy and Hewlett Johnson, The Socialist Sixth of the World: the first by a party member, the second by the archetypal fellow-traveller. The chapter headings of Sloan's book, written in 1937, suggest we are in utopian territory. These include 'Equality of Opportunity', 'The Rights of the Wage-Earner', 'The Power of the Trade Unions', 'A People's Press', 'A Workers' State' and 'A Socialist Constitution'. We are told, for example, that 'Forced Labour, terrifying as it may sound, is . . . in fact . . . the imposition of a fine, on the instalment system'[23] and that 'compared with the significance of that term in Britain, Soviet imprisonment stands out as an almost enjoyable experience'![24] On the question of freedom of the press Sloan asserts that:

> the working citizen of the U.S.S.R. enjoys an effective freedom of expression, in two ways, which is not enjoyed by him [sic] in other countries. First, the material in the newspapers is what he writes, and not what a privileged few

write for his consumption. Secondly, what he writes is effective in the sense that it leads to concrete action being taken against abuses, bad practices, inefficiency, and injustice . . . The Soviet Press can truly claim to be democratic.[25]

This, it should be noted, was written in a period when the Stalinist terror had assumed new barbaric proportions. Having crushed the party, the machinery of repression set to work on the population as a whole. This was the classic period of the knock on the door in the middle of the night, followed by torture, a summary trial (often none at all), foul imprisonment and, frequently, death. Cultural and intellectual life was dead, as were many of its practitioners. A democratic press there was not!

Hewlett Johnson's book was published in 1939. He greatly admired the notion of five-year plans, an enthusiasm he attributed to Soviet citizens in general:

The successive Five-Year Plans are awaited with an eagerness unbelievable here. No financier ever hung on the declaration of the budget with half the zest that the common man in the Soviet Union awaits the publication of the Five-Year Plan. It constitutes the standard, the goal, the charter, the incentive, and the stimulus for millions of Soviet citizens.[26]

The Soviet Union, we are told, has virtually established the first stage of socialism/communism:

The completed socialist system of society automatically creates the classless society, and with the abolition of classes the need for one class to predominate ceases.

That stage has been largely completed within the brief space of twenty-one years.[27]

The road to the next stage beckons. As to Stalin, nothing could be further from the truth than that he is a dictator. Rather, he is the kind and noble shepherd of his people, gently leading them to the promised land:

Stalin is no oriental despot. His new Constitution shows it. His readiness to relinquish power shows it. His refusal to add to the power he already possesses shows it. His willingness to lead his people down new and unfamiliar paths of democracy shows it. The easier course would have to add to his own power and develop autocratic rule. His genius is

> revealed in the short, simple sentences which enshrine the Basic Law of the U.S.S.R. . . . Here is a document which ranks amongst the greatest in all human documents in its love of humanity and its reverence for human dignity.[28]

And so on and so on. Randomly dipping into this literature simply reveals more of the same.

It would be wrong to get too self-righteously censorious about these writers. They were neither stupid nor insincere – quite the reverse. Easy hindsight neglects the objective problems these people faced – limited access to information, a hostile political climate, etc., etc. Nor is their response a mere historical curiosity. The desire to see ideals realized is both deep and recurring. This is especially the case where it seems that the realization is occurring in under-developed, previously exploited areas. All the complex motives of the friends of the Soviet Union have reappeared since in respect to China, Vietnam, Kampuchea, Cuba, Latin America and so forth. Did the radical enthusiasm for the Chinese Cultural Revolution adequately grasp at the time the realities of that phenomenon? How do you register support for a new revolution without, on the one hand, falling into uncritical sycophancy, or, on the other, playing into the hands of the interests of reactionary capitalism? This is a fiendishly difficult question to answer. It is too easy to mock the supporters of the Soviet Union. They had no historical experience to draw upon. We do and have often done no better.

The whole utopian edifice came crashing down in 1956, with Krushchev's denunciation of Stalin and the Soviet suppression of the Hungarian uprising. Well before this, however, disillusionment had set in – with major cracks appearing in the structure. Particularly damaging were the denunciations of ex-communists. 1947 saw the publication of *I Chose Freedom* by the Soviet defector, Victor Kravchenko. In this indictment of the Soviet Union by an ex-official, Kravchenko sarcastically referred to the utopian cult of Stalinist Russia in the west:

> The Stalinist propaganda in the outside world had been more successful than any of us in Russia suspected. The myth of a happy 'socialist' land is treated as a grim piece of totalitarian ballyhoo inside Russia; it is accepted literally, solemnly, in an almost religious transport of faith by a large part of those men and women who create public opinion in the outside democratic world.[29]

'*The God That Failed* appeared in 1950. In it, six prominent writers: Arthur Koestler, Ignazio Silone, Richard Wright, André Gide, Louis Fischer and Stephen Spender, related their initial enthusiasm for, but eventual disenchantment with, communism. The same type of word crops up throughout: 'illusion', 'fanaticism', 'duped' and 'dictatorship'. Koestler, who was in the party in the thirties, conveyed how Stalinism both drew on the personal spring of idealism and poisoned it:

'The addiction to the Soviet myth is as tenacious and difficult to cure as any other addiction. After the Lost Weekend in Utopia the temptation is strong to have just one last drop, even if watered down and sold under a different label'.[30]

Douglas Hyde's *I Believed: The Autobiography of a former British Communist* appeared in 1951.[31] Hyde aired many of the grievances that were to become commonplace amongst current and former party members after 1956: the cynicism of the party; the constant recourse to blatant lies; hyper-centralism; Soviet domination of the party; the strait-jacket policy in eastern Europe. In Hyde's case there was a rejection of the entire vision of Marxism, as he understood it, and its replacement with Roman Catholicism. Stalinism's fall was clearly in danger of bringing Marxism down with it. Some party members sought to distinguish authentic Marxism from Stalinism; firstly inside, but often ultimately outside, the party. Thus E. P. Thompson in 1956 put his finger on the authoritarian utopianism at the heart of Stalinism:

Stalinism is socialist theory and practice which has lost the ingredient of humanity. The Stalinist mode of thought is not that of dialectical materialism, but mechanical idealism . . . Stalinism is Leninism turned into stone . . . Instead of commencing with facts, social reality, Stalinist theory starts with the idea, the text, the axiom: facts, institutions, people, must be brought to conform to the idea . . . Stalinist analysis, at its most degenerate, becomes a scholastic exercise, the search for 'formulations' 'correct' in relation to text but not to life.[32]

There were also Marxists who had never been within the fold of world communism, for whom the revelations merely confirmed what they had long known. What is impossible to quantify is the injury done to Marxism – and to socialism – by the exposure of

Stalinist utopianism. The great ideals of communism were now associated with concentration camps, secret police and tanks. An ideal stick had been fashioned for the right to use.

3) The stick was eagerly grasped. A whole generation of conservative and cold-war liberal theorists constructed their critique – and at the centre of most lay a particular interpretation of utopianism. Reduced to its bare bones, the argument went thus:

a) individuals experience hardship in their lives.
b) They are therefore prepared to listen to people who offer them the vision of a life without hardship.
c) The new system ends up with even greater hardship than the old one.
d) Therefore put up with inevitable hardship (or at most aim for some mild amelioration of this condition) and don't listen to the siren voices of utopians.

J. R. Talmon's *The Origins of Totalitarian Democracy* (1952) sought to chart the origins of this repressive approach to politics. It arose because people did not realize the limits to felicity: 'Totalitarian democracy early evolved into a pattern of coercion and centralization not because it rejected the values of eighteenth-central liberal individualism, but because it had originally a too perfectionist attitude towards them'.[33] To overcome this it is necessary

> to attack the human urge which calls totalitarian democracy into existence, namely the longing for a final resolution of all contradictions and conflicts into a state of total harmony. It is a harsh, but none the less necessary task to drive home the truth that human society and human life can never reach a state of repose. That imagined repose is another name for the security offered by a prison, and the longing for it may in a sense be an expression of cowardice and laziness, of the inability to face the fact that life is a perpetual and never resolved crisis. All that can be done is to proceed by the method of trial and error.[34]

Thus we can see the service rendered by Stalinism in allowing Talmon plausibly to erect this caricature of the radical and socialist vision – he may be referring to earlier dictatorships but his readership knew full well his actual target. He can thus import his own ideal, his own utopia – and all the value-laden and questionable assumptions underpinning it – under the rubric of realism, and relegate Marxism to mere utopianism. The experience of Stalinism also allowed theorists of 'totalitarianism' such as Friedrich and Brzezinski to equate fascism and communism, where the latter was used to include any but the most bland forms of socialism.[35] The political use of George Orwell's dystopias is also instructive. The US right in particular portrayed *Animal Farm* and *Nineteen Eighty-Four* as attacks on socialism itself. But, as Bernard Crick shows in his fine biography, Orwell wanted to distinguish clearly between Stalinism and socialism. Thus he wrote, in a preface to *Animal Farm*: 'for the past ten years I have been convinced that the destruction of the Soviet myth was essential if we wanted a revival of the socialist movement'.[36] Nor did Orwell subscribe to the characteristic anti-utopianism of this period. He was gloomy about the modern world, but this didn't involve a rejection of Utopia, as he made clear in a review of 1946:

> The 'earthly paradise' has never been realized, but as an idea it never seems to perish, despite the ease with which it can be debunked by practical politicians of all colours.
>   Underneath it lies the belief that human nature is fairly decent to start with, and is capable of indefinite development. This belief has been the main driving force of the Socialist movement, including the underground sects who prepared the way for the Russian revolution, and it could be claimed that the Utopians, at present a scattered minority, are the true upholders of Socialist tradition.[37]

Frederic Warburg, the publisher of *Nineteen Eighty-Four*, reveals, in a summary of the book, both the common misinterpretation of the work and the political climate eager to misinterpret:

> The political system which prevails is Ingsoc = English Socialism. This I take to be a deliberate and sadistic attack on socialism and socialist parties generally . . . and it is worth a cool million votes to the Conservative Party; it is imaginable that it might have a preface by Winston Churchill after whom its hero is named.[38]

Post-war social democracy was also able and willing to make political capital out of the experience of Stalinism. They saw it as a vindication of their gradualist and reformist political strategy. Revolutionary Marxism led to the prison camp and tyranny and as a result had been exposed in its true light. Thus social-democrats were now able to portray their particular vision of socialism as realistic and democratic and lump anything more radical in with the category of utopianism, fanaticism or totalitarianism. Shirley Williams can therefore claim that the 'one essential difference between social democrats and Communists is that social democrats never swallowed the millennialism that was implicit in Marx'[39] and then proceed to attack 'Utopians, purists and revolutionaries who prefer their socialism untrammelled by the responsibilities of government'.[40]

The Soviet experience therefore raises the issue of utopianism in a number of forms. The revolution was initially castigated as 'utopian' by those who argued that Russia's backward conditions were alien terrain for a socialist society. Others have seen the Bolshevik move as a triumph of forward thinking, of creative politics. The early years of the revolution certainly saw a great explosion of utopianism; one pole being the need for back-breaking development, the other that of intoxication with a limitless future. Under Stalin, authoritarian utopianism came into its own, committed to overcoming Soviet backwardness in a context of international isolation. This approach, with all its accompanying deceptions, was able to capture the fund of goodwill to the USSR in the west. The phenomenon of 'Russia as utopia' was the result. The reality, when discovered, broke many people's hope and, despite valiant attempts by non-Stalinist Marxists, provided a field-day for those who had most to gain from a retreat from vision. As we shall see in Chapter 8 the passing of Stalin did not signal the end of Marxist-Leninist authoritarian utopianism. The establishment of the 'People's Democracies' in the post-war period stimulated in time a Marxist counter-attack which was not afraid to deploy a radical utopianism against its authoritarian opponent.

CHAPTER 6

ERNST BLOCH AND THE UBIQUITY OF UTOPIA

In the next four chapters we shall look at the attempts made by four twentieth-century Marxists to highlight the utopian dimension in Marxism. We shall begin with Ernst Bloch (1885–1977),[1] whose work represents a magnificent attempt to develop a self-consciously utopian Marxism. In numerous weighty tomes Bloch hammered home the centrality of the utopian for any rational politics. His masterpiece is undoubtedly *The Principle of Hope*, initially written, over nine years (1938–47), in American exile and revised in the 1950s. We shall follow the structure of this work to get to grips with Bloch's main themes.

THE PRINCIPLE OF HOPE

For Bloch, the enemies of hope are confusion, anxiety, fear, renunciation, passivity, failure and nothingness. Fascism was their apotheosis. But since all individuals daydream, they also hope. It is necessary to strip this dreaming of self-delusion and escapism, to enrich and expand it and to base it in the actual movement of society. Hope, in other words, must be both educated and objectively grounded; an insight drawn from Marx's great discovery: 'the subjective and objective hope-contents of the world'.[2]

The Principle of Hope is an encyclopaedic account of dreams of a better existence; from the most simple to the most complex; from idle daydreams to sophisticated images of perfection. It develops a positive sense of the category 'utopian', denuded of unworldliness and abstraction, as forward dreaming and anticipation. All the time, however, the link between past, present and future is stressed – concern with what one might be is the royal road to what one has been, and what one is: 'we need the most powerful telescope, that of polished utopian consciousness, in order to penetrate precisely the nearest nearness'.[3] This whole project is examined under five headings, each referring to a distinct form of hope:

1 'Little Daydreams': all those flights of fancy and reveries that occupy people throughout their day.
2 'Anticipatory Consciousness': the very basis of hope; the roots and purpose of dreaming in the individual.
3 'Wishful Images in the Mirror': the expression of hope in such forms as display, fairy tale, travel, film and the theatre.
4 'Outlines of a Better World': planned or outlined utopias – medical, social, technological, architectural and geographical utopias, plus the 'wishful landscapes' of painting and literature.
5 'Wishful Images of the Fulfilled Moment': the most powerful conceptions of authentic humanity.

'Little Daydreams'

This delightful little section examines, with great sensitivity and acuity, a range of everyday hopes and fantasies. Bloch vividly recaptures the dreams of childhood: the secure hiding places, voyages to exotic lands, far-away castles, unlimited power; also the adolescent fantasies of love where the 'street or town in which the loved one lives turns to gold, turns into a party',[4] or the dream of returning home in triumph to the once unfeeling, but now awestruck, parents. Ever mindful of the experience of fascism, Bloch notes how these early yearnings were often captured, how the 'often invoked streak of blue in the bourgeois sky became . . . a streak of blood'.[5] With maturity comes the wishful rewriting of history, where the wrong turn is righted and the missed opportunity achieved, and related to this is the dream of revenge. With great personal bitterness, Bloch evokes the murderous, anti-semitic fantasies of the petit-bourgeois in the Weimar Republic and of their cynical manipulation by the bourgeoisie. He also details the various compensatory sexual fantasies of individuals: 'a dream forest of randy eyes and spread legs',[6] and the visions of financial success and domestic comfort. The inevitable limitations of bourgeois dreaming are emphasized – and most graphically exemplified in the figure of the jaded and bored rich man who has had the misfortune (to use Shaw's phrase) to get his heart's desire. By contrast, what Bloch terms the 'non-bourgeois dreamer', looks beyond the existing range of options to the socialist vision of true equality, freedom and community. Inevitably, these yearnings are 'considerably less distinct than those which need only reach into the existing window-display'.[7] They are, however, of a much higher status, and represent the way forward. This leads on to Bloch's touching and bittersweet account of the dreams of old age, where he contrasts the unnecessary hardship of the old under capitalism with the vision of wisdom and rest, evening and house, of 'authentic life in old age'.[8] Throughout this section on little daydreams one is struck by powerful images and evocative phrases: of how, for the young visitor to the big city, 'the houses, the squares, the stages seem bathed in a utopian light',[9] or of the brutality, malice and repulsiveness of petit-bourgeois dreams 'as pervasive as the smell of urine',[10] or, again of this latter class: 'it is also quite happy to put its clenched fist back into its pocket when crime is no longer allowed a free night on the town by those at the top'.[11]

'Anticipatory Consciousness'

In this section Bloch goes back a stage and seeks to establish the basis of human dreaming, human aspiration: the basis, in other words, of hope. He distinguishes a whole series of interlinked tendencies within the individual – urging, striving, longing, searching, driving, craving, wishing and wanting – all of which propel us beyond ourselves. But what is behind these? He rejects the various Freudian explanations of motivation: they are saturated with bourgeois assumptions; they are oriented to the past ('there is nothing new in the Freudian unconscious');[12] they are obsessed with the libido ('it emphasises solely spicey drives';)[13] they disembody human impulses and consequently ignore basic socio-economic factors, and fail to grasp the historical mutability of human drives. Freud's one-time disciples come in for particular condemnation; Adler's 'will to power' is dismissed as an apology for capitalism, whilst Jung, that 'fascistically frothing psychoanalyst',[14] is accused of a racist and irrational primevalism. A much better candidate for a basic drive, Bloch argues, is hunger, 'the drive that is always left out of psychoanalytic theory',[15] and, as regards 'complexes', he suggests 'the one which Franziska Reventlov so unmedically called the money complex'.[16] Both rest on the only real basic drive – self-preservation – though even this is experienced differently in different environments. Self-preservation, however, turns into self-extension, as basic appetites are satisfied and give way to ever more sophisticated forms; ultimately, 'out of economically enlightened hunger comes today the decision to abolish all conditions in which man is an oppressed and long-lost being'.[17] Dreaming is an integral part of this process. Bloch is at pains to counter Freud's minimizing of the differences between day-time and night-time dreaming. Although wish-fulfilment occurs in nocturnal dreams, it is in an essentially regressive, repressive and highly distorted form. Daydreams, by contrast, combine clarity, open-endedness and future orientation. However, even the dreams of the night contain material which can be transformed into a utopian form in waking consciousness. The crucial element in all of this is what he terms the 'Not-Yet-Conscious'. This is a pre-conscious faculty in individuals, from which all novel material is generated: it is 'the psychological birthplace of the New'.[18] The New, however, does not come out of the blue, nor is it pure subjective creation; rather, it is drawn from the objective possibilities of the developing real world: 'inspiration . . . emerges . . . from the meeting of subject and object, from the meeting of its tendency with the objective tendency of the time, and is the flash with which this concordance begins'.[19] Only in Marxism is there this combination of hope and concreteness. This involves a combination of the 'warm stream' and the 'cold stream' of Marxism, where coldness is the rigorous scientific aspect and warmness its libertarian intent; this is expressed elsewhere as the unity of sobriety and enthusiasm. Again, there is much more in this section than this very bare summary suggests. Throughout, Bloch branches off into all manner of fascinating discussions – from art to folklore, history to religion; philosophy to psychology – in which he deploys a truly awesome erudition (as well, let it be said, as a deal of pomposity and wilful obscurity). This whole section, of nearly three hundred pages, is the theoretical core of Bloch's project. The underlying ideas are attractive. The concept of the 'Not-Yet-Conscious' avoids much of the insulting reductionism present in Freudian psychology. Its image of the individual is not that of the battered and screwed-up end-product of obscure childhood traumas, but of a person endowed with much greater independence and capacity for creative self-development. Instead of brooding on the hidden – and usually base – roots of people's desires and wishes, it focuses on the desirability of the goals and the beneficial function of the dreams. It also lends itself much more readily to an overall Marxist framework than do attempts to harness Freud to this end. On the other hand, sceptics might reply that this is due to the highly general and abstract nature of the concept 'Not-Yet-Conscious': its reliance on the author's intuition and on cultural authorities – the fact, in short, that it hasn't deigned to soil its hands with the clinical procedures of the Freudians.

'Wishful Images in the Mirror'

This is an exciting, original and important section. Bloch's achievement is to have uncovered the utopianism in (the often despised) mass or popular culture. He is fully aware of the exploitative nature of this culture, but equally of its link with wish-fulfilment (again, these are not always healthy wishes). As he notes of fashion and display:

> people cannot make of themselves what has not already previously begun with them. Equally, in terms of pretty wrappings, gestures and things, they are attracted outside only by what has already existed for a long time in their own wishes, even if only vaguely, and what is therefore quite willingly seduced. Lipstick, make-up, borrowed plumes help the dream of themselves, as it were, out of the cave. Then they go and pose, pep up the little bit that is really there or falsify it. But not as if it were possible for someone to make themselves completely false; at least their wishing is genuine.[20]

The travelling fair and circus also, amidst their tackiness and exploitation of the not-normal, are said to contain 'a bit of frontier land . . . with preserved meanings, with curiously utopian meanings, conserved in brutal show, in vulgar enigmatic-ness'.[21] Bloch shows the influence of his beloved Karl May in his assertion of the utopian content of adventure tales – a genre which is a 'castle in the air *par excellence*, but one in good air and, as far as it can be true at all of mere wishing-work: the castle in the air is right'.[22] Our author casts his net far and wide for vehicles of wishing such as, for example, travelling, stamp collecting, gardening, delight in wild weather. Dance 'paces out the wish for more beautifully moved being';[23] mime points to another region, as does film. Here again, the double-edged nature of the phenomenon is stressed: Jitterbug and Boogie-Woogie are 'imbecility gone wild'[24] and Hollywood is condemned as 'Dream-factory in the rotten . . . sense'.[25] But rotten dreams are not the ultimate enemies: those enemies are, rather, pessimism and nihilism – the absence of dreams:

> artificially conditioned optimism . . . is nevertheless not so stupid that it does not believe in anything at all . . . For this reason there is more possible pleasure in the idea of a converted Nazi than from all cynics and nihilists . . . Thus pessimism is paralysis *per se*, whereas even the most rotten optimism can still be the stupefaction from which there is an awakening.[26]

In the 1930s, Bloch had analysed the paradoxical nature of fascism – its mixture of the progressive and the reactionary. This was due to the fact that 'not all people exist in the same Now'.[27] Many sections of the population carried within themselves consciousness from earlier times because they were not fully integrated into contemporary society. Fascism managed to harness these older currents to its own chariot. Marxists, on the other hand, failed to see the progressive dimension in elements of this earlier consciousness; failed to see that these elements were produced by inadequacies in earlier societies. These elements are the

> still subversive and utopian contents in the relations of people to people and nature, which are not past because they were never quite attained . . . These contents are, as it were, the gold bearing gravel in the course of previous labour processes . . .[28]

Socialists cannot simply dismiss the whole phenomenon, they must attempt to integrate this valid dimension into their politics. As Bloch concluded at the time, fascism will continue 'as long as the revolution does not occupy and rebaptize the living Yesterday'.[29] Socialism, the ultimate goal, can therefore draw upon myriad sources deep in every individual. This is Bloch's great service in this section: he points to a transmission belt between the small-scale, the mundane – and even the seemingly reactionary – and the grand *telos* of communism. Where one might fault him is in his rather arbitrary distinctions between authentic and inauthentic: where, for example, adventure stories are placed on a higher footing than 'syrupy stories' in glossy magazines. This was due partly to an inevitable personal quirkiness, plus the broader influences of the milieu in which he grew up. There does also appear to be in these distinctions a strong dose of the anti-Americanism found in many of the 'emigration' generation of Weimar Germany. There is some loss of sensitivity as a result. This, however, is only a minor caveat; the overall perspective is truly impressive.

'Outlines of a Better World'

In the nearly five hundred pages which make up this section, Bloch assembles the different conscious attempts to depict a better world – the more usual meaning of the word 'utopia'. There are the various medical utopias, deeply rooted in perennially human concerns, with their abolition of disease and pain. However, even the perennial is rooted in a particular historical context – 'utopias have their timetable',[30] Bloch insists, and they cannot be understood outside their time. We are then treated to an encyclopaedic account of historical utopias. Along with the usual Plato we get Solon, Diogenes and Aristippus. The Bible is seen as a treasure-house of utopian imagery; Moses is credited with the creation of a liberation God: 'the God he imagines is . . . no masters' God . . . Yahweh begins as a threat to the Pharaoh: the volcanic God of Sinai becomes Moses' god of liberation, of flight from slavery'.[31] Jesus is interpreted as the harbinger of a new world: 'the eschatological sermon has precedence for Jesus over the moral one and determines it'.[32] Augustine is included, as is the fascinating medieval heretic Joachim of Fiore, with his dream of the Third Kingdom. And so on, through More and Campanella, Rousseau and Fichte, Owen and Fourier, Cabet and Saint-Simon, past Stirner, Proudhon and Bakunin, on to Weitling. He includes a rather odd section of women's utopias, which many modern feminists would find patronizing and sexist, as they would many of his references to women throughout the work. He claimed that the women's movement 'is at once outmoded, replaced and postponed',[33] in that capitalism is more than willing to extend its worthless equality and class struggle has primacy over sexual struggle. It is, however, only postponed in that women have a utopian dimension to contribute to future socialist society, a contribution defined in terms of the 'special qualities' of women. This gives way to a discussion of Zionist visions ('Zionism flows out into socialism, or it does not flow out at all'),[34] then the utopian works of Bellamy, Morris, Carlyle and George. The account is seemingly endless: technological utopias, architectural utopias from 'Dreams on the Pompeian wall' to Le Corbusier, geographical utopias ('Eldorado and Eden'), wishful landscapes in painting, opera and literature ('Pieter Brueghel painted his Land of Cockaigne exactly as the poor folk always dreamed it to be')[35] and so on and so on. The erudition and colossal scale are quite breathtaking. It is an absolute gold mine for those interested in utopias. Bloch's purpose, however, is not antiquarian – rather it is both to demonstrate the historical ubiquity of this type of dreaming forward and to argue for a synthesis of dreaming, stripped of illusion, with a Marxism stripped of positivism and empiricism, where 'everything inflamed in the forward dream is thereby removed as is everything mouldy in sobriety'.[36] This is the concept of 'concrete utopia'.

'Wishful Images of the Fulfilled Moment'

In this concluding section, Bloch presents what he considers to be the most sublime images of existence, the ones which throughout history have possessed an aura of profound otherness. These are the golden seams of human dreaming. They also provide a window on the deepest beliefs and values of Bloch himself. Historically, these images have often appeared in contradiction to one another: contradictions which will develop into dialectical syntheses. Thus there will be a life combining the old opposed ideals of danger and happiness, in which courage and adventure prevent enervation and boredom, and felicity prevents brutality, insecurity and emptiness; there is the new tactical ideal of 'neither non-violent hesitation nor cunning abstractness of violence, but violence concretely mediated'.[37] The same is said of the other dualisms – body and soul, action and contemplation, solitude and friendship, individual and collective. Two important areas of focus in this section are music and religion. The notion of art as a bridge to an order outside and beyond the given has a long history; so too has an appreciation of the subversive role of art. The exalted status of poetry in classical Greece is well known, as is Plato's desire to control it in his ideal society. In modern times, Schiller developed the concept of art as a vehicle for a normative ideal – a standard from which to criticize current arrangements and a goal for political change. For Bloch, music, like all phenomena, has an ideological dimension, rooted in its time: 'it extends from the form of the performance right to the characteristic style of the tonal material and its composition, to the expression, the meaning of the content. Handel's oratorios in their festive pride reflect rising imperialist England . . .'.[38] This does not exhaust its content, for as Bloch argues elsewhere:

> a 'significant' work does not perish with the passing of time, it belongs ideologically, not creatively, to the age in which it is socially rooted. The permanence and greatness of major works of art consists precisely in their operation through a fulness of pre-semblance and of realms of utopian signifi-cance.[39]

In fact, 'no art has so much surplus over the respective time and ideology in which it exists'[40] as music. The complex qualities of music have made it a particularly rich vehicle for the expression of utopian content and historically it has expressed the most sublime longings of humanity: 'thus music as a whole stands at the frontiers of mankind'.[41] Bloch attempts the (as he would himself admit) impossible task of articulating some of these images of liberation. In the case of religion we are dealing with a phenomenon which has been looked down on in the Marxist tradition. It is sometimes forgotten by Marxists that Marx's remark that 'religion . . . is the opium of the people' occurs in a passage where the critical element of religion is also referred to: religion, for Marx, is also 'the sigh of the oppressed creature';[42] it is 'the expression of real distress and the protest against real distress'.[43] That this was forgotten in the Marxist tradition is no doubt due to Marx's own opinion that religion's critical moment had passed – that it had nothing further to contribute to a revolutionary politics. Bloch, on the other hand, develops an impressive analysis of the critical and anticipatory elements in the world's religions and argues for the continuing relevance of religion in Marxism. The religious impulse, stripped of its illusory aspects, is thus profoundly revolutionary. This involves:

the elimination of God himself in order that precisely
religious mindfulness, with hope in totality, should have
open space before it and no ghostly throne of hypostatis. All
of which means nothing less than just this paradox: the
religious kingdom-intention as such involves atheism, at least
properly understood atheism.[44]

or, as he pithily put it later: 'Only an atheist can be a good
Christian, only a Christian can be a good atheist'.[45]

The book throughout displays Bloch's pro-Soviet Marxism-
Leninism. Thus we are informed that 'The Soviet Union faces no
question of women's rights any more, because it has solved the
question of workers' rights'[46] (and he doesn't mean by abolishing
them!) and that the Soviet Union is in the forefront of progress
across the board. This was a long-standing theme in Bloch's
work. He defended the Moscow Show Trials in 'A Jubilee for
Renegades' (1937). Of the critics, 'the renegades', he wrote:

> Although many of them have loved the beginning of
> the Russian Revolution, during the last two years they have
> lost their enthusiasm. They cannot get over the fact that this
> 20-year-old bolshevist child must rid itself of so many
> enemies, and that it discards them so ruthlessly.[47]

After the war, Bloch accepted a university post in East Germany
at Leipzig, and for a number of years appears to have found
nothing particularly objectionable in the Marxist-Leninist concept of the communist party. In a lecture to an East German
audience he couched his utopian perspectives in the language of
Marxist-Leninist planning:

> adventure is in the vanguard of the dialectical-material
> process, together with a plethora of real problems which
> evoke courage in order to survive the venture, as well as
> penetratingly concrete reason – needed in order to perceive
> the tendency. This wisdom, the always keen and well-
> thought-out wisdom of Lenin, watches over the path to the
> classless society. Out of this non-schematic approach new
> intermediate analyses of situations, always more concrete
> and expanded two-year, five year plans of theory and
> practice are always arising.[48]

The party would thus appear to be the ultimate directional force,
the guardian of analysis and utopia. On such puny legs,

therefore, did Bloch rest his great edifice. In the wake, however, of party harassment and revelations of the nature of Soviet Stalinism, Bloch became disillusioned and in 1961 took up permanent residence in West Germany. In his new home he argued that Marxism's own shortcomings had enabled the authoritarian centralism of Stalinism to triumph. Neglect of the natural law tradition had resulted in concern with human happiness not being matched by concern for human dignity:

> There are men [sic] who toil and are burdened, those are the exploited. But in addition there are also men who are degraded and offended . . . The factor of vexation and degradation urgently deserves a name and a concept. Stalinism was able to impose itself without resistance because this term was hardly heard in Marxism after 1917.[49]

Another lacuna, present in Marx's own work, was a 'comparatively weak emphasis on personal freedoms'[50] which assisted the anti-democratic nature of Stalinism. Bloch cites Rosa Luxemburg's slogan 'No socialism without democracy' as an example of a healthier trend.

This then is Bloch's great masterpiece. His achievement was to see that utopianism is not confined to intellectuals and their various blueprints of a better life. He saw that, in countless ways, individuals are expressing unfulfilled dreams and aspirations – that in song and dance, plants and plaster, church and theatre, utopia waits.

CHAPTER 7

HERBERT MARCUSE TURNS
TO SIGMUND FREUD

With Herbert Marcuse (1898–1979)[1] we encounter a number of the themes treated in Bloch's work. Unlike Bloch, however, Marcuse was deeply influenced by Freud's work and sought to enrich his own distinctive utopian Marxism from this source. In the 1930s, prior to his intensive study of Freud, the clear utopian dimension of his thinking is apparent in his discussion of fantasy.

FANTASY

In a 1937 essay, 'Philosophy and Critical Theory', Marcuse pointed to the potentially progressive role of fantasy in Marxism. Fantasy can be the bridge between the irrational present of capitalism and rational communism. Mere conceptual thought, by contrast, is unable to make this leap: 'The abyss between rational and present reality cannot be bridged by conceptual thought. In order to retain what is not yet present as a goal in the present, phantasy is required'.[2] He cites Aristotle and Kant on the power of the imagination to intuit that which is not there; to create novelty out of the given; to be free in the midst of unfreedom. The temptation to imagine anything, no matter how fantastic or irresponsible, need not be succumbed to, for Marxism 'does not envisage an endless horizon of possibilities'.[3] Reality itself establishes the parameters of responsible imagination – it establishes the agenda for what is possible and what impossible: 'The freedom of imagination disappears to the extent that real freedom becomes a real possibility. The limits of phantasy are . . . technical limits in the strictest sense. They are prescribed by the level of technological development'.[4] His conclusion is unambiguous: 'In a situation where such a future is a real possibility, phantasy is an important instrument in the task of continually holding the goal up to view'.[5]

By the 1950s Marcuse had grounded the concept of fantasy in his radical Freudianism. At first sight, Freud seems a most improbable basis on which to build a utopian social theory. His work abounds with gloomy and pessimistic statements about the need for considerable repression and renunciation in any conceivable society. For Freud, civilization has been built on 'the suppression of instincts',[6] as individuals have renounced pleasure and curbed their antisocial desires. In *The Future of an Illusion* he sketches out a future golden age, in which coercion and the suppression of the instincts disappear, and comments: 'it is questionable if such a state of affairs can be realized. It seems rather that every civilization must be built upon coercion and renunciation of instinct'.[7] Elsewhere, in reply to Einstein's question 'Why War?', he said of the claim that 'there are races whose life is passed in tranquillity and who know neither coercion nor aggression': 'I can scarcely believe it';[8] and to the claim of the Soviet Union that it would cause aggressiveness to disappear by the abolition of scarcity and the establishment of equality he said bluntly: 'That in my opinion is an illusion'.[9] Marcuse, however, claimed to find a revolutionary core in Freud's work centred on his theory of the life instinct Eros. The concept of fantasy is reintroduced into this new theoretical context. Fantasy is now said to act in the service of the id and its 'pleasure principle'. It champions in various forms all that is most authentic in humanity against the restrictions of the 'performance principle'. It returns that which is repressed in the present:

> Freud's metapsychology here restores imagination to its rights. As a fundamental, independent mental process, phantasy has a truth value of its own – namely, the surmounting of the antagonistic human reality. Imagination envisions the reconciliation of the individual with the whole, of desire with realization, of happiness with reason.[10]

One example Marcuse cites is the role of fantasy in the so-called perversions. Imagination is an integral part of the 'perverse' revolt against the unfree organization of sexuality in modern society and it prefigures the libidinal freedom of future rational society. In art, also, the 'return of the repressed' is manifest – its imaginative structures make liberation a temporary reality and a possible goal. 'In a less sublimated form', Marcuse adds, 'the opposition of phantasy to the reality principle is more at home in such sub-real and surreal processes as dreaming, daydreaming, play, the "stream of consciousness" '.[11] Throughout this analysis there is a stress on the role of memory as a link between past gratification and its future possibility which recalls that 'primitivism' discussed in a previous chapter.

MEMORY

As Marcuse was well aware, the notion of the power of memory had an ancient pedigree. In the Orphic mysteries of ancient Greece the soul of the departed was warned to avoid the spring of forgetfulness, Lethe, and instead approach the spring of memory, Mnemosyne, and say to its Guardians:

> I am a child of Earth and of Starry Heaven; But my race is of Heaven (alone). This ye know yourselves. And lo, I am parched with thirst and I perish. Give me quickly the cold water flowing from the Lake of Memory.[12]

In this way salvation could be obtained. This myth in turn influenced Plato. In his *Meno*, Socrates contends that 'seeking and learning are in fact nothing but recollection'[13] and bases this claim on the argument that the immortal soul carries the knowledge acquired in earlier reincarnations. In the *Republic*, in the celebrated myth of Er, the ability to resist drinking the water of Lethe is seen as a measure of philosophical and moral development. All who are condemned to return to earth must drink of forgetfulness (the foolish drink the most) – only those free of the cycle of rebirth (or who are messengers of the divine, such as Er) will retain remembrance.[14] The mechanisms of memory and forgetfulness were at the heart of Freud's project. He sought to show that the act of forgetting is often a form of defence against the intolerable – and memory the road to overcoming the resulting neurosis. He vigorously opposed 'the error of supposing that the forgetting we are familiar with signified a destruction of the memory trace'[15] and asserted the contrary: 'the primitive stages can always be re-established; the primitive mind is in the fullest meaning of the word, imperishable'.[16] He also, in a way that was to influence Marcuse, speculated about the continuing presence in contemporary individuals of 'memory-traces' of the experience of earlier generations.

For Marcuse, memory is the means to recapture earlier experiences of freedom and happiness. It is a way of thwarting any attempt to eternalize existing unhappiness. By showing that happiness once obtained, it also raises the possibility of, and the desire for, future satisfaction. This is the 'truth value' of memory:

> Its truth value lies in the specific function of memory to preserve promises and potentialities which are betrayed and even outlawed by the mature, civilized individual, but which had once been fulfilled in his [sic] dim past and which are never entirely forgotten . . . Against the self-imposed restraint of the discoverer, the orientation of the past tends towards an orientation on the future. The recherche du temps perdu becomes the vehicle of future liberation.[17]

In outlining this revolutionary function of memory, Marcuse, in effect, attempts to combine the foci of the historical approach of the Golden Agers *and* the psychological approach of Sorel. He wishes to link 'the origin of the repressed individual' (ontogenesis) to 'the origin of repressive civilization' (phylogenesis) and he says of fantasy that 'it preserves the archetypes of the genus, the perpetual but repressed ideas of the collective and individual memory, the tabooed images of freedom'.[18]

At the collective level, Marcuse utilizes Freud's depiction of prehistoric society, which he accepts cannot be factually corroborated, but argues that 'the alleged consequences of these events are historical facts'.[19] Freud's hypothesis has 'symbolic' value through dramatizing and explaining the basis of human history. It is essentially a story of paternal domination giving way to maternal liberation – only to be overthrown itself by a new paternalist domination. The primal father's monopoly of sexual pleasure provokes an act of patricide by his sons, but the moment of liberation rapidly gives way to a new restrictive order as a response to the emergence of guilt. And yet the memory of gratification will not go away: it has perennially reappeared throughout history as an indictment of – and target for – the forces of repression. At the individual level, Marcuse follows Freud in positing 'an impression of the past in unconscious memory traces' whereby 'concrete and tangible factors . . . refresh the memory of every generation'.[20] In other words, he believes in the reappearance in the individual of an archaic heritage in which domination confronts liberation and believes also that this heritage is 'awakened' by experiences such as the Oedipus complex which parallel ancient experiences. In every generation, therefore, the developing individual experiences gratification which, like the archaic inheritance, continues to haunt the 'mature' years. The collective heritage therefore coexists with the individual experience of childhood and infantile gratification. Again, fantasy provides access to this treasure trove:

> phantasy . . . retains the structure and the tendencies of the psyche prior to its organization by the reality, prior to its becoming an 'individual' set off against other individuals. And by the same token, like the id to which it remains committed, imagination preserves the 'memory' of the subhistorical past when the life of the individual was the life of the genus, the image of the immediate unity between the universal and the particular under the rule of the pleasure principle.[21]

Such memory is a spur to change; it is an actual and powerful goad to re-create the lost conditions of happiness, for 'the past continues to claim the future; it generates the wish that the paradise be re-created on the basis of the achievements of civilization'.[22]

The corollary to this is that forgetfulness – amnesia – can be a powerful weapon in the armoury of existing society. 'The ability to forget', says Marcuse, 'is the mental faculty which sustains submissiveness and renunciation'.[23] By forgetting one both loses the imagery of liberation and forgives that which should not be forgiven. In *One Dimensional Man*, Marcuse cites Adorno's fear of 'The spectre of man without memory'[24] as bourgeois society seeks to neutralize history. In so far as memory is cultivated, it is in the repressive form of memorizing the requirements of the capitalist order – what Marcuse calls 'the one-sidedness of memory-training in civilization', where 'the faculty was chiefly directed toward remembering duties rather than pleasures; memory was linked with bad conscience, guilt and sin. Unhappiness and the the threat of punishment, not happiness and the promise of freedom, linger in memory'.[25] Memory triumphs over repression's greatest ally, time, by not allowing it to conceal either the dark or the light: 'Time loses its power when remembrance redeems the past'.[26] In this respect Marcuse was particularly struck by Benjamin's claim that, in the July Revolution in France, a number of the revolutionaries shot at the public clocks.

It might be noted in passing that Freud's own work provides a classic example of the treacherous nature of memory, its intimate link with fantasy and the capacity for self-delusion in those involved in interpreting memory. For years he believed that neurosis was generated by the sexual seduction of children, on the basis of the so-called 'memories' of his patients. Only later did he realize that in many cases this 'memory' was a fantastic and highly repressed report of quite different events.

REGRESSION

Given Marcuse's concern with the collective and individual past of humanity, it is not, perhaps, surprising that he envisages the future partly in terms of regression. Now for Freud regression was a purely negative phenomenon. It was a reversion to immature levels and could often, as in psychotic fantasies, lead to profound mental illness. His was the spirit of Paul of Tarsus: 'When I was a child, I spake as a child, I understood as a child, I thought as a child: but when I became a man, I put away childish things'. The expression 'savages or children' flowed easily from Freud's pen. For Marcuse, by contrast, a more appropriate text might perhaps be that from Matthew's Gospel: 'Except ye be converted and become as little children, ye shall not enter into the kingdom of heaven'. A truly civilized society will have to regain those features which time and maturity have eradicated. He makes this quite clear in *Eros and Civilization*:

> the emergence of a non-repressive reality principle
> involving instinctual liberation would *regress* behind the
> attained level of civilized rationality. This regression would be
> physical as well as social: it would reactivate early stages of
> the libido which were surpassed in the development of the
> reality ego, and it would dissolve the institutions of society in
> which the reality ego exists. In terms of these institutions,
> instinctual liberation is relapse into barbarism.[27]

Although at pains to deny that barbarism in the pejorative sense will occur, the 'primitive' aspects of his vision are in no way concealed. Thus, when looking for an illustration of the new relationships that will obtain between humanity and nature, he turns to the work of the anthropologist Margaret Mead. Her work on the Arapesh is cited, with its description of this people's conception of the world as a garden. Likewise, Marcuse uses Freud's work on infantile sexuality in his anticipation of the resexualization of the body and in a sense looks forward to a return to infancy:

> The regression involved in this spread of the libido would first manifest itself in a reactivation of all erotogenic zones and, consequently, in a resurgence of pre-genital poly-morphous sexuality and in a decline of genital supremacy. The body in its entirety would become an object of cathexis, a thing to be enjoyed – an instrument of pleasure.[28]

However, this is not simple revivalism. Marcuse is not envisaging a total return to the past but rather an enrichment from the past on the basis of all that is best in modernity. Future society will thus be a synthesis of the 'primitive' and the 'advanced':

> It would still be a reversal of the process of civilization, a subversion of culture – but *after* culture had done its work and created the mankind and the world that could be free. It would still be 'regression' – but in the light of mature consciousness and guided by a new rationality. Under these conditions, the possibility of a non-repressive civilization is predicated not upon the arrest, but upon the liberation of progress.[29]

ART

Much of the previous analysis figures in Marcuse's work on art. This was a theme which fascinated him throughout his life, from his doctoral thesis on artist-novels to his last published book, *The Aesthetic Dimension*. In the 1930s he had spoken of great art as a repository of images of liberation and quoted Schiller's lines: 'What we have here perceived as beauty/We shall some day encounter as truth'.[30] He was, like Bloch, equally aware of the power of art to affirm the status quo – and this perception of the double-edged quality of art surfaces throughout his subsequent work. Art's link with fantasy and memory is stressed and it too is given a psychological grounding. Art has the power to create alternatives to the present. Great bourgeois art has historically 'held up . . . as a task the image of a better order',[31] it has placed a question mark over the given by its evocation of the beautiful other. Art is, therefore, one of the most potent forms of imagination. It is also a form of memory, recalling a beauty that once was and which might once more be. Not surprisingly, Proust's *A la recherche du temps perdu* exercised a particular fascination for Marcuse. Such art derives its power from the creative, erotic, life instinct; it is therefore firmly based in a level of fundamental truth in the individual. 'In the aesthetic imagination', says Marcuse, 'sensuousness generates universally valid principles for an objective order'.[32] In the late 1960s, when Marcuse was most dismissive of affirmative bourgeois culture, the 'primitive' dimension of his work was most apparent in his discussion of art. He saw in black music an oppositional eroticism that was prior to, or outside, bourgeois society and the bourgeois individual:

> They now oppose . . . their own music, with all the defiance, and the hatred, and the joy of rebellious victims, defining their own humanity against the definitions of the masters . . . In the subversive, dissonant, crying and shouting rhythm, born in the 'dark continent' and in the 'deep South' of slavery and deprivation, the oppressed . . . give art a desublimated, sensuous form of frightening immediacy, moving, electrifying the body, and the soul materialized in the body.[33]

Throughout his work on art, Marcuse resists vulgar Marxist attempts to reduce art to mere ideology. He rejected approaches which tried to read off art from class or held naive conceptions of 'political art'. Although his views on particular forms changed over the years, a common thread was that good or authentic art was political – even if there was no explicit political content, or even if the artist held conservative views. Similarly, ideological soundness was no guarantee of genuine (and therefore political) art – and could very often destroy the political impulse by its political nature. Thus, writing in the 1970s, in the hangover period after the party of the late 1960s, he says:

> The most uncompromising, most extreme indictment has found expression in a work which precisely because of its radicalism repels the political sphere: in the work of Samuel

Beckett, there is no hope which can be translated into political terms, the aesthetic form excludes all accommodation and leaves literature as literature. And as literature, the work carries one single message: to make an end with things as they are.[34]

UTOPIA

Given Marcuse's orientation to the future, it is not surprising that he wishes to make his position on utopianism clear. In particular, he wanted to denounce the ideological misuse of the term 'utopian' by those who wished to equate the undesirable (from their point of view!) with the impossible. In a lecture given in 1967, entitled 'The End of Utopia', he argued that the word 'impossible' could have two possible meanings in connection with utopia. In the first case 'the impossibility of realizing the project of a new society exists when the subjective and objective factors of a given social situation stand in the way of the transformation';[35] when, in other words, there are socio-political obstacles to the new society. The other use is when a project 'contradicts certain scientifically established laws, biological laws, physical laws';[36] when it is, strictly speaking, physically impossible. He argued that it is only in this second sense that the word 'utopia' can be used today. The first type of project 'can at best be designated only as "provisionally" unfeasible'[37] because:

1 unfeasibility only manifests itself after the fact; novelty is merely untried, not untriable;
2 unfeasibility fixes the present; it assumes that the current balance of forces is eternal.

If the material and intellectual basis for the new society exists – and Marcuse does consider this to be the case – the failure to establish this society is a political matter and has nothing to do with possibility versus impossibility. It is in this sense that Marcuse refers to the 'end of utopia'.

Marcuse also, however, wished to use 'utopian' in a positive sense to refer to all those impulses and aspirations which have been blocked by existing society. This involved a rejection of positivism and scientism wherever it occurred, including Marxism. Thus, in rejecting Marx's conception of the relationship between the 'realm of necessity' and the 'realm of freedom', he noted 'the possibility that the path to socialism may proceed from science to utopia and not from utopia to science'[38] and it was in connection with this point that he spoke of 'passing from Marx to Fourier'.[39] In *An Essay on Liberation*, this position is forcefully argued:

> Up to now, it has been one of the principal tenets of the critical theory of society (and particularly Marxian theory) to refrain from what might be reasonably called utopian speculation . . . I believe that this restrictive conception must be revised . . . What is denounced as 'utopian' is no longer that which has 'no place' and cannot have any place in the historical universe, but rather that which is blocked from coming about by the power of the established societies.[40]

In short, Marxism is not utopian enough!

ABOVE AND BELOW

Underlying Marcuse's often-criticized wide range of revolutionary subjects (blacks, hippies, students, women, etc., etc.) is the conviction that capitalism does produce its own gravediggers. Whatever his views on the proletariat, he shares with Marx the belief that the very 'success' of capitalism simultaneously undermines it. In particular, capitalism generates a desire for socialism. On the one hand there are all those who are excluded from the benefits of capitalism and experience that absolute want which was once the lot of the classical proletariat. Like these predecessors, they have many dreams of plenty and abundance: some reactionary in nature, but some which embody the traditional values of socialism. In the Third World and in the poverty of the First, Marcuse saw one pole of the opposition to capitalism. To this was added the sickened beneficiaries of the system whose very affluence had generated transcendent needs – needs that capitalism is incapable of satisfying. An unintended consequence of capitalist productivity has been the production of dreams of a pollution-free environment, of male and female equality, of new work patterns – of, in effect, the replacement of capitalism by socialism. It was always Marcuse's hope that these two poles could in some fashion come together as a broad anti-capitalist front. That this was only a hope reflects his awareness of the countervailing forces at work, most graphically described in *One Dimensional Man*. It was this which provided the political space in his work; the need for an agency to encourage the naturally self-destructive tendency of capitalism. His mature preference was for a non-Marxist-Leninist, anti-authoritarian agency: one that would act as a 'catalyst' on the oppositional currents in society. Only in this way could the goal of the movement, socialism, be operative in its means.

PROBLEMS

The danger inherent in the use of the concept of 'false consciousness' is graphically demonstrated in the work of Marcuse. Starting from the proposition that people do not necessarily know their own minds, he develops a sweeping condemnation of contemporary needs and desires. Whole areas of modern culture are deemed to involve deluded complicity with the system, whether it be liking certain forms of entertainment; desiring certain products, or dreaming certain dreams. Politics is collapsed into aesthetics as a particular definition of 'good taste' is raised to the purple of 'correct consciousness'. A fondness for Nabokov's *Lolita* rather than Tolstoy's *Anna Karenina* is a manifestation of one's shallowness, as is a preference for the television over the opera. A liking for plastic is a sign of serious mental ill-health, as is a delight in noisy, crowded museums, transistor radios and the streets of Manhattan. In a manner reminiscent of Bloch at his worst, the complexity of human aspiration is swept away before a highly subjective universalization of the culture of the German intellectual. This is surely at the root of the appalling lack of predictive power in Marcuse's work, in that a society which was said to be almost terminally afflicted with 'one dimensionality' in 1964 could display such vigour in 1968. Was there no connection between the liberalization of sexual mores dismissed as 'repressive desublimation' in *One Dimensional Man* and the moral/sexual rebellion celebrated in *An Essay on Liberation*? This is a serious flaw in Marcuse's work.

Another problem lies in his commitment to Freud. Freud offered that heart's desire of any Marxist – a material grounding for socialism. Here was a biological base for reason which promised a 'rationality of gratification'. Every individual had a spark of the divine in them which could illuminate the way to the New Jerusalem. Marcuse has, however, laid himself open to attack on two fronts. Many have taken issue with his radicalized Freud which, it has been argued, violates the unity of the Freudian system. In particular, critics have argued that the conservative cast of Freud's work is not some kind of unnecessary optional extra that can be jettisoned at will without the whole being undermined. Also, time has not been particularly kind to Freud's later metapsychology, upon whose highly speculative propositions Marcuse relied heavily. By bravely throwing in his lot with the Freudian hypotheses he inevitably cut a rod that could be used on his own back. Not that Freud has been 'disproved', for he is not that type of thinker – his psychology is closer to a social science, with its methodological 'problem' of unfalsifiability, than it is to a natural science. In any case, the libertarian and utopian cast of Marcuse's thought was established long before the Freudian infusion. In his Hegelian Marxism of the 1930s we have all the elements of fantasy, memory, art and utopia. At the very least, if one is worried about the 'scientific' status of all Freud's hypotheses, one might still see them as a type of social poetry dramatizing and emphasizing Marcuse's utopian project.

CHAPTER 8

RUDOLF BAHRO: EAST AND WEST

The work of Rudolf Bahro[1] (born 1935) spans two very different worlds. He grew up in East Germany where, particularly after the invasion of Czechoslovakia, he developed a penetrating Marxist critique of the repressive institutions of Soviet societies; as a part of this process he created a highly distinctive form of utopianism. In the wake of the trouble this caused him with the authorities he moved to West Germany, where he became deeply involved with the new Green Party. His utopianism registered the change. Bahro's thought must be seen as a powerful and original contribution to the whole question of a Marxist utopianism. Let us start with the radical Marxist currents of eastern Europe.

EAST EUROPEAN MARXISM

Critical east European Marxists are confronted with societies claiming to be advanced on the road towards communism. In a sense they face the question of what is to be done when one is unhappy in a place that purports to be utopia, or if not utopia then at least its antechamber. It is not surprising, therefore, that analyses have arisen which highlight the failings of the authoritarian utopianism of orthodox Marxism-Leninism. This sense that something has gone badly wrong, and that urgent solutions are required, comes out very clearly in a remark by the Hungarian Mihaly Vajda:

> Marx's critics sketched the picture of marxist socialism as a negative utopia which humanity should not bring into being. The fact that the marxist utopia was realized in the negative

form drawn by its critics presents us socialists with new theoretical tasks.[2]

Many found Marxism inadequate to the task and moved into different ideological territory. Many of those who tried to rejuvenate Marxism fell foul of their respective governments and experienced exile or worse. It will come as no surprise, therefore, that much of their criticism is highly circumspect and often takes the form of analyses of other countries and other times, or speaks of 'tendencies' and 'dangers': an element of decoding is therefore often required.

The Polish Marxist Adam Schaff has written of the contradiction between individual needs and party plans of the good life, between the pluralism implied in the former and the centralism of the latter:

> Since the feeling of happiness is always an individual
> sensation, which is organically bound to the psychophysical
> structure of the perceiving subject, any attempt to settle the
> problem in a 'general' way, by means of sweeping definitions,
> or even worse, by laying down when and in what circum-
> stances people *should* be happy is doomed to failure; and in
> the case of a state embarking on *practical* activity to this effect,
> it may bring real human misery.[3]

Schaff enlists the help of the dystopian novelists Zamyatin and Orwell to make his case. Their writing takes 'to their logical extreme some of the tendencies in socialist ideology and certain developments in socialist countries, and thus helps us better to visualize the dangers'.[4] His conclusion is that, whilst it is possible to state what the causes of *unhappiness* are, such a possibility is lacking with respect to *happiness*. Schaff is also critical of the exalted claims made in utopianism – its promise of worldly bliss without end – and one senses here a reaction to official rhetoric. He argues that 'even in ideal social and economic conditions people can individually be unhappy – no economic or social system can protect them against disease, the death of their near ones, unrequited love, personal failures, etc'.[5] It is for this reason that he asserts: 'Marxist humanism does not promise any utopian paradise and does not claim to provide a key to individual happiness for everybody'.[6] A recurring criticism is that the 'goals' established for eastern Europe are simply the inappropriate imposition of the experience of the Soviet Union. The first 'proletarian revolution', it is argued, took place in a backward, foreign land, early in the century, and cannot be simply grafted on to the very different conditions of contemporary eastern Europe. This is often accompanied by a call for a 'national road to socialism'. The undemocratic nature of the whole process is often stressed – as, for example, in the simple lack of popular input, or where the notion of the 'ultimate goal' becomes a fig leaf for anti-democratic acts. The Yugoslav Veijko Korác analyses the way in which Stalinist bureaucracies use the notion of 'the ultimate goal' to legitimate both their own privileged position and the relative deprivation of the population as a whole:

> The high ethical standards of socialism are misapplied for entirely profane purposes, most often for those purposes that correspond to the interests of the bureaucracy, which thinks only of itself and identifies that self with society and socialism, speaking of an ideal future while enjoying *today's* pleasures and considering itself the single interpreter of historical laws . . . In Stalinist practice, faith in socialism was transformed into one of the main levers of despotic arbitrariness which, in the name of certain 'greater' future goals, and the 'future happiness of humanity,' became antihuman and anticritical in the highest degree, until it finally turned into ruthless state idolatry.[7]

The rich conceptual framework of Marxism has been ossified into bureaucratic clichés. Even where the bureaucracy is not corrupt, it is infected with that lack of vision so prevalent amongst earnest reformers. One is reminded of Tom Paine's observation on the Quakers:

> Though I reverence their philanthropy, I cannot help smiling at the conceit, that if the taste of a Quaker had been consulted at the creation, what a silent and drab-coloured creation it would have been! Not a flower would have blossomed its gaieties, nor a bird been permitted to sing.[8]

The various writers speak of the widespread cynicism such developments have engendered. The mixture of ignorance, caution, hostility and cynicism is, at times hilariously, conveyed in a transcript from Radio Budapest, printed in *Encounter*. A reporter in Karl Marx Square asked passers-by who Karl Marx was:

A: Oh don't ask me such things.
Q: Not even just a few words?
A: I'd rather not, all right?
Q: Why not?
A: The truth is, I have no time to study such things.
Q: But surely you must have heard something about him at school?
A: I was absent a lot.
Another Voice: He was a Soviet philosopher.
Another Voice: Of course a politician. And he was, you know, he was what's his name's – Lenin's, Lenin, Lenin's works – well, he translated them into Hungarian.

People were also asked whom Engels Square was named after:

A: After Engels.
Q: And who was Engels?
A: He was an Englishman, and he screwed around with Communism.
[Laughter]

Q: Do you remember his other name?
A: Engels, Engels . . . Marx Engels, Marx, wasn't it?

Q: Where did Engels live?
A: He lived in Leningrad, that is, in Moscow.

Q: Do you know whom Engels Square was named after?
A: I don't know. I am not from Budapest. I don't know.[9]

The whole language of 'final goals', especially in its Marxist form, has fallen into disrepute. From the perspective of the ordinary worker the minority of people who use such language are either fools or hypocrites. No link is established between his/her own aspirations and this hollow metaphysics of ends.

Authoritarian utopianism is, however, quite unable to smother alternative forms of utopianism. A classic example is provided in Miklós Haraszti's account of a Hungarian factory, *A Worker in a Worker's State*. One of the principal consolations for workers in the oppressive conditions of the factory is the production of 'homers'. These are small, not particularly useful objects, made out of scrap material, secretly produced in snatched free moments. Haraszti sees in the passionate addiction of the workers to the production of these little trinkets an elementary form of autonomy and transcendence. It is the workers' 'loophole to happiness':[10]

> This humble little homer . . . is the only form possible of free and creative work – it is both the germ and the model: this is the secret of the passion.
> The tiny gaps which the factory allows us become natural islands where, like free men, we can mine hidden riches, gather fruits and pick up treasures at our feet. We transform what we find with a disinterested pleasure free from the compulsion to make a living.[11]

One might also speculate in this vein on the role of religion in recent Polish history. Although there is clearly much that is reactionary in Polish Catholicism – and many other reasons why people might embrace it – none the less, one might postulate a utopian function for it. Jean-Yves Potel, in his study of the Solidarity period, *The Summer Before The Frost*, sees in the recourse to religion a utilization of an alternative source of imagery, values and hope against the party and its barren ideology:

> The language and concepts of Marxism were changing meaning. They now bore the mark of a totalitarian power. A song that had now become dry, boring and outdated . . . So it is not surprising, in such conditions, that the words which, in Western Europe, express the hopes of a left-wing move-ment, are here kicked in the gutter, trampled underfoot by a working class which can at last shout aloud what it thinks and what it wants. Where is it supposed to go in search of another language, in other symbols and other heroes? It will go to what survives in its memory. To that tradition which bureaucratic domination has not been able to kill. To that culture which, despite everything, has remained alive. One sole institution has kept sufficient strength and sufficient tradition for this – the Church.[12]

Also, some east European Marxists have not moved from a condemnation of authoritarian utopianism to a condemnation of all forms of utopianism. The Hungarian, Agnes Heller, one of the Budapest school, has never been afraid to stress the need for a future orientation. For Heller, the future is sufficiently open to admit of a number of alternatives and this places on the present generation the responsibility of thinking about, and choosing between, the various options. No magical recourse to the march of history or vague injunctions to extrapolate from current trends can remove this responsibility. She employs a Blochian distinction to highlight the beneficial dimension in Marx's own work:

> Engels spoke with pride of the development of socialism from utopia to science. Today, science contains more than a few utopian elements. But as Ernst Bloch has so strikingly said, there are fertile and infertile utopias. There are many respects in which Marx's ideas on the society of associated producers and on the system of needs of united individuals are utopian, when measured against our own today and our own possibilities for action; they are none the less fertile. He establishes a norm against which we can measure the reality and value of our ideas, and with which we can determine the limitedness of our actions: it expresses the most beautiful aspiration of mature humanity, an aspiration that belongs to our Being.[13]

Likewise, two other members of the school, Maria Markus and Andras Hegedus, reject the two extremes of 'voluntarism', which neglects the real world and speaks of iron laws independent of the human will, and 'scientistic planning', which uses scientific procedures in pursuit of narrow political goals. Instead, like Heller, they conceive of the future as both conditioned and open:

> The future, as far as we are concerned, is therefore not some sort of system or chain of necessary events which can be discovered in advance, but the result of human activity which, though limited in a certain way at every given historical moment, is not unequivocally determined.[14]

Morality, that dirty word in Marxism, thus has an important role to play.

Bahro's *The Alternative in Eastern Europe* (written 1972–77 and described by Marcuse as 'the most important contribution to Marxist theory and practice to appear in several decades')[15] contains both the negative and positive dimensions previously discussed: it presents a nuanced and sophisticated analysis of the malaise of eastern Europe and speculates on possible sources of transcendence in a distinctly utopian vein. Bahro brought to his text the knowledge of an insider. He was for many years a loyal, though far from uncritical, member of the party and served it in a number of full-time capacities (newspaper editor, trade union official, etc.). His growing fears about party rigidity came to a head with the Warsaw Pact invasion of Czechoslovakia. This provided the stimulus to the labour which eventually brought forth *The Alternative*. His starting point is the discrepancy between the image of liberation outlined in Marx, which is nominally subscribed to by the party élites in the communist world, and the sad reality of these 'socialist' societies. A reactionary bureaucracy has come into being; the bourgeois state form has not been smashed; the traditional division of labour still exists; great social inequalities obtain; money, commodity, production and wage labour still exist; the abolition of private property has led, not to its socialization, but to its monopolization by the bureaucracy; puritanism abounds; socialist ideology repels thought rather than stimulating it; the political system is obsolete and socialist 'nations' relate as antagonists. The resulting crisis in these societies is, for Bahro, a classic example of relations of production acting as a fetter on the forces of production. The roots of this lie in the fact that, whereas Marx conceived of socialism as building on the abolition of capitalist property, the Soviet 'non-capitalist' road initially emerged in a society with minimal capitalist property. In Marx's scenario, socialism would reap the benefits of bourgeois society – the Bolsheviks lacked this vital base. The October revolution was the first anti-imperialist revolution, in a country with a half-feudal, half-Asiatic socio-economic structure. The only way the revolution could survive was through a powerful state building up the productive forces. Terror and bureaucracy, themselves deeply rooted in Russia's past, were inevitable outcomes of this attempt to establish the preconditions of socialism. Today, however, the various forms which sustained the Soviet revolution in its early years now block further development. This is especially the case in countries like Bahro's own, East Germany, and Czechoslovakia, where this alien Soviet model was superimposed on a very different historical experience.

One can see the attraction of this approach to the 'problem' of Soviet societies. It takes seriously the Marxist concern with the broader socio-economic context and avoids the 'great individuals' approach underpinning the explanatory notions of crazed dictators and wicked bureaucrats. However, it is a hazardous approach for someone like Bahro who will later argue for the importance of the subjective factor in his utopian strategy. We are asked to believe, for example, that, 'if a more gifted man than Stalin' had been in control, 'Russia would have been spared the Caesarian madness, but hardly more'.[16] This is dangerous stuff, reminiscent of the 'great slaughter bench of history' type of determinist explanation. It plays into the hands of the very bankrupt Marxism-Leninism he is at such great pains to counter.

As the title of Bahro's book suggests, there is an alternative to the current state of affairs. This, as ever in Marxism, prompts Bahro to confront the category 'utopian'. His conclusion is significant:

> Marxists have a defensive attitude towards utopias. It was so laborious to escape from them in the past. But today utopian thought has a new necessity. For that historical spontaneity that Marx conceived as a process of natural history and which our Marxist-Leninists celebrate in the name of objective economic laws, *must* be overcome.[17]

This initially involves the reassertion, in all its radicalness, of the vision of general emancipation enunciated by Marx and Engels – the vision of fulfilled individuals freed from all the old constraints on further development. In turn, this vision has to be concretely created. No amount of talk about economic laws can obscure the necessity of the subjective factor in this transformation. Bahro believes that this subjective dimension can come from what he terms 'surplus consciousness', 'an energetic mental capacity that is no longer asorbed by the *immediate* necessities and dangers of human existence and can thus orient itself to more distant problems'.[18] In other words, society has sufficiently conquered scarcity that it releases mental space for the noble work of achieving human fulfilment. The revolutionary task is to accelerate this process.

> The problem is to drive forward the 'overproduction' of consciousness, so as to put the whole historical past 'on its head', and make the idea into *the decisive* material force, to guide things to a radical transformation that goes still deeper than the customary transition from one formation to another within one and the same civilization. What we are now facing, and what has in fact already begun, is a *cultural*

revolution in the truest sense of the term: *a transformation of the entire subjective form of life of the masses* . . .[19]

Bahro is absolutely clear that the old Marxist idea of the proletarian revolution is obsolete in both the capitalist and non-capitalist world. The demand of general emancipation can no longer be exclusively grounded in a specific social class or stratum: 'we need *the creation of an overwhelming* – even if formally eclectic – *consensus for solving the general crisis, the constitution of the party with its mass following reaching into all social strata as the general representative of a new order*'.[20] This is not simply good strategy; it also reflects the authentic idea of humanity.

A very personal part of Bahro's vision of socialism is its ecological dimension. He rejects the technological/industrial idea of progress which is dominant in the modern world. It is a selfish and destructive concept which helps perpetuate all the other types of oppression in society. A break has to be made with such ways – future society will have to be 'simpler' or it will not be able to exist at all:

> *The communist association, as a social body that will be master of its problems without having to strangle its individual members, can only be a system of quantitatively simple reproduction, or at most very slow and well thought out expanded reproduction, of men [sic], tools and material goods.*[21]

To the idea of limitless external exploitation, Bahro counterposes the 'journey inwards'.[22]

Bahro conceptualizes the new revolution as the 'overcoming of subalternity',[23] where subalternity is defined as 'the form of existence and mode of thought of "little people" '.[24] He outlines five goals to overcome this:

1 A redivision of labour whereby there is both variety and equality in labour.
2 Unrestricted access to general education.
3 Enlightened education of children.
4 A new, fulfilling, communal life.
5 'the socialization [democratization] of the general process of knowledge and decision'.[25]

This would be utopianism in the pejorative sense of the word if it were simply a matter of wishing. The whole project has to be objectively grounded – it must have an active subject:

Without this, the proposal would be no more than a personal illusion. Only if what is necessary and possible shows itself to be a field of needs, demands, and compulsions requiring action by concrete social forces, are we faced with a genuine perspective.[26]

Such a base does exist. The events in Czechoslovakia in 1968, the Prague Spring, are interpreted by Bahro as living proof of the forces for change in eastern Europe: 'It became evident then . . . that actually existing socialism [his term for Soviet societies] generally *does* contain a latent bloc of interests directed against the existing political regime'.[27] In particular, there was developed in surplus consciousness the vital emancipatory interests. These emancipatory interests are defined thus:

> There are recognizable barriers from which men have always
> sought to emancipate themselves, in order to obtain access to
> something, and appropriate something, that is conceived
> time and again in the ideas of freedom, joy, happiness, etc.,
> which no cynical irony can expunge. The inexhaustible
> possibilities of human nature, which themselves increase
> with cultural progress, are the innermost material of all
> utopias, and moreover a very real, and in no way immaterial
> material at that. They inevitably lead to the desire to
> transform human life.[28]

In Czechoslovakia, these interests were so mobilized that it took the tanks of the Warsaw Pact to restore a bogus normality.

The experience of Czechoslovakia underlined for Bahro the inevitable intellectual-led nature of fundamental opposition in eastern Europe. This, he says, is not a demand but a simple reality. Factors such as differential education and work patterns of necessity place intellectuals in the forefront of social change. Nor need this lead to the imposition of the special group interests of the intellectuals on society, for intellectuals can articulate the universal and general interests of the whole society. Such intellectuals will form the core of the embryonic League of Communists proposed by Bahro. This organization is seen as an alternative to the ruling communist party. Although Bahro is sensitive to the rigidities of the existing party, he insists that a party form is still required to mobilize the progressive forces in the society. Although at some future stage different forms may become appropriate, in the immediate future 'there is still need of a leading communist party'.[29] In all of this the cloven hoof of Bahro's Marxist-Leninist past is apparent. His explanation of why there can only be *one true party* taps into that reservoir of vulgar determinism which fed his account of Soviet history. There cannot be a multiplicity of parties, he argues, because: 'A plurality of political parties rests on a class structure consisting of clearly different and even contrary social elements',[30] and he grandly states that 'the conception of party pluralism seems to me an anachronistic piece of thoughtlessness'![31] Although his conception of the new party is admirably open and flexible, this blinkered rejection of party pluralism undermines his theory of transformation.

THE WEST

After a period of imprisonment resulting from the publication of his book, Bahro went to live in West Germany. In an interview with *New Left Review*, he reflected on his relationship with Marxism. To be a Marxist in eastern Europe is 'like being a Christian in the Middle Ages':[32] Marxism is the intellectual universe; its frameworks and assumptions are the air intellectuals breathe. Bahro saw his previous role as a heretic, but one of the same faith – 'Luther against the Pope'.[33] 'But here in the West', he said, 'I find myself forced more and more often to say I am no longer a Marxist . . . There are many particular elements in Marx that I still find useful, but the structure itself I have abandoned'.[34] His new political self-description was perhaps predictable: 'From scientific socialism I have returned to utopian socialism'[35] (though he also expressed unease about the term 'socialism'). In part this reflects Bahro's move from a society where Marx was God Almighty but, more importantly, it also reflects a number of perceived fundamental disagreements with Marxism, many already present in *The Alternative*.

The ecological sentiments of *The Alternative* now come centre stage. These are said to be the key to the only authentic radical theory and practice. The ecology crisis is where 'all the contradictions of the prevailing mode of production and way of life, all the dangers of the world situation, intersect and coalesce'.[36] In this spirit, Bahro threw in his lot with the West German Green Party, arguing at its founding congress in 1980 that this was the only sensible thing a socialist could do. Marx is now shown the inadequacies of his critique, his alternative and his theory of transition. Perhaps we can imagine Bahro addressing Marx on these matters:

The Critique. *You are wrong, Marx, both to overestimate and underestimate the importance of capitalism. You overestimate it by not realizing that capitalism is merely the latest phase of a much deeper malaise – the inherently exploitative nature of European civilization. This civilization, throughout its history has been destructive of both humanity and nature. You therefore underestimate the dangers of capitalism in your belief that all that is required is a revolution in social relations – apart from this it is business as usual. Examine the great religions of ancient Asia and you will discover a qualitatively superior reality principle.*

The Alternative. *Your vision of communism does not fundamentally break with the old repressive society. Communism, as you conceive it, still seems to me to be a wasteful industrial society geared to the production of useless products for unnecessary needs. My vision of the future stresses simplicity, the small-scale, the non-industrial, the internal rather than the external. All your talk about objectification and labour reveals to me how much you are still in thrall to the continuum of repression.*

The Theory of Transition. *How can you believe that the working class will liberate humanity? The working class is in many ways the most compromised social group in capitalism. It has an insatiable appetite for the production of capitalism, and has internalized to its very core the values of this system. In so far as it has a class mission it is for greater and greater consumption, not the ending of exploitation. Real emancipation requires that people rise about their class nature – the only genuine revolutionary subject is humanity.*

From the various collections of speeches, interviews, etc. which have been published in the past few years, we can see Bahro attempting to develop strategies and tactics for his revolutionary ecology. Throughout, his preference is clearly for the extra-parliamentary dimension of the Greens; his suspicions of the parliamentary wing, particularly their proneness to the danger of systemic co-option, are never far from the surface. He believes that the Greens can win over the surplus consciousness of people across the political spectrum. As an example of this he cited the experience of a friend:

he told me . . . about his brother's wife, now middle-aged and bound up in typically Bavarian middle-class ways,

perhaps lower middle class . . . He always thought of the
wife as conservative, Catholic and so on, but to his surprise
she voted for the Greens . . . particular motives functioned
differently in that case. Some relationships shifted, without
the things which had always made her vote for Strauss
suddenly disappearing from her head.[37]

Bahro has been particularly keen on the establishment of
alternative communes, which, with his ever-growing interest in
religion, he sees in terms of a 'new Benedictine order'.[38] Thus
there is a return to the old Owenite prefigurative strategy. He
has also been heavily involved in peace and anti-nuclear
politics. Capra and Spretnak, in their study, *Green Politics*, say of
Bahro that 'he has purposely not organized any cadre around
himself and considers his role to be that of a "visionary and
prophetic Green" '.[39] They also note: 'We were surprised . . . to
see his mild-mannered demeanour give way to a style of public
speaking that can become quite animated and intense'.[40]
Unfortunately for Bahro, his worst fears were in the end realized
– the Greens, in his opinion, succumbed to the status quo. He
resigned from the party in 1985, with bitter words:

> The Greens have identified themselves – critically – with the
> industrial system and its political administration. Nowhere
> do they want to get out. Instead of spreading consciousness
> they are obscuring it all along the line. They are helping to
> patch up the cracks in the general consensus.[41]

Bahro's experience in the west has been one of trying to
develop an alternative to his abandoned Marxism. The eclecticism
of his recent work reflects his painful process of building. His
problems are immense. How can he link his highly personal,
and rather ascetic, utopia to an analysis stressing the thoroughly
corrupt and fragmented nature of contemporary society? Two
immediate problems suggest themselves. Firstly, his is not a
pluralist approach to utopia. He has a clear outline of what is
desirable and little tolerance for those who propose significantly
different models. Can one build a mass movement with these
exclusivist assumptions? Isn't this a repeat of the problem in *The
Alternative*, where an attack on the authoritarian utopianism of
Marxism-Leninism itself culminated in a rather rigid emancipatory structure – The Communist League? This is compounded
by the fact that many of the main planks of Bahro's vision are

not, one suspects, immediately attractive (what, for example, will be made of his assertion that 'Perhaps it will be adequate if we travel to Italy [only] twice, as Goethe did'[42] or his remark: 'In a sense, the commune perspective I advocate for the developed countries would involve us in becoming something like the Third World'?[43]). Secondly, his position is reminiscent of Marcuse in his highly pessimistic *One Dimensional Man* – society is so rotten, in its culture, values, institutions – even in its oppositional movements – that one wonders where liberation can come from? Even the Greens let him down!

None the less, the concluding lines of his letter of resignation end on a note of both hope and defiance:

> I wouldn't consider it right just to withdraw silently. I am not becoming unpolitical. I am not saying goodbye to the intellectual process. I want to contribute to creating a new place and a new practice. Clearly we have to take a longer run-up. We must risk some cold water if we want to assemble the necessary substance for our withdrawal from the industrial system, first of all within ourselves.[44]

We await his next phase with interest.

CHAPTER 9

ANDRÉ GORZ

In a recent work of Gorz[1] (born 1924), the book's title, subtitle and principal heading eloquently reveal the writer's utopian credentials. The title is *Paths to Paradise*; the subtitle, 'On the Liberation from Work' and the principal heading, 'Twenty-five theses towards understanding the crisis and finding a Left solution'. The book's target is the 'realism' of the left, its retreat to the failed practices of the past in the face of present disintegration. The left, he says, 'is clearly about to die from lack of imagination'.[2] In such a situation, the genuine realist is the utopian. The utopian is fixated on neither the past nor the present, but rather grasps the future in its still-embryonic form in the present: 'There are times when, because the social order is collapsing, realism consists not of trying to manage what exists but of imagining, anticipating and initiating the potential transformations inscribed in present changes'.[3] Thus we see once more this distinctive idea of Marxist utopianism. Let us now try and see on what foundations *Paths to Paradise* is built.

THE SIXTIES

In the mid sixties, Gorz was influenced by a number of contemporary Italian Marxists, such as Basso and Trentin, who advocated industrial democracy and workers' control. His commitment to this type of strategy rested on a broader belief that workers must develop an alternative to the present to become truly revolutionary. No reliance can be placed on some kind of unconscious collision between forces and relations of production. There has to be a 'long period of anti-capitalist struggle conducted with a sense of the true purpose of work and life'[4] and this necessarily includes 'a comprehensive concept of post-capitalist society.'[5] This can occur initially only at the point of production, where the workers both experience the cutting edge of exploitation and exist as a potentially powerful group. The logic of the resulting strategy is that low-level and particularist demands concerning work conditions, etc. can develop into ever higher and more radical objectives: for worker control of management, for the suppression of capitalism and so forth. In this way, the bogus collectivity of the bourgeois state and the economic system it reflects will be replaced from below by these new tiers of social and political democracy. Mindful, no doubt, of the dangers of 'economism', Gorz sees the need for a 'mass party' to help radicalize the workers. He is, however, emphatic that this cannot be a Bolshevik party, since that was the product of backwardness and has no place in an advanced society. Thus, whereas the Bolsheviks were primarily concerned with the repressive functions of the state, the modern party will initially attack the state's political/ideological functions. Furthermore, the modern party does not face an undeveloped mass but a relatively sophisticated work force – the old strategy of inducing consciousness from without has therefore been rendered obsolete:

> The party must no longer be a vanguard separate from the masses or an organization detached from the struggle, but an active element within the masses which, like a ferment, stimulates action wherever this is possible, helping the masses to create their own organs of struggle and collective leadership, and to achieve the political vision implied by the carrying of their own experience to its logical conclusion.[6]

Centralism is a necessary evil in the party – it will perish after the bourgeois state has been destroyed.

The notion of the relatively sophisticated work force is a part of the 'new working class' theory associated with Serge Mallet and with Gorz. The increasingly technical nature of capitalism has resulted, Gorz argues, in a greater need for workers with a higher educational level. The working class is thus expanding to include intellectualized proletarians and proletarianized intellectuals. Such workers are much more likely than the old working class to disengage creatively from capitalism. A consequence of this is that the gap between manual and theoretical, intellectual and labourer, student and worker, have been lessened. This paves the way for political co-operation between these historical antagonists. Capitalist attempts to introduce specialized technical training to counter this process are doomed, because 'one cannot teach knowledge and ignorance at the same time':[7]

> The capitalist dream of a specialized technician who will combine a passion for his work with total indifference to the ends it serves, professional initiative with social acquiescence, a sense of responsibility in technical matters with irresponsibility in the social and economic field, is one that cannot be realized.[8]

Traditional education was also undergoing a transformation during this period. Capitalism's need for an educated work force had resulted in great expansion in education. Increased numbers led to increased competition for jobs, which in turn led to many using their new intellectual skills against the existing order. With higher education no longer guaranteeing status and security, students were becoming increasingly radicalized. The whole caste-ridden nature of education was under attack. The form, content and purpose of education was being questioned. This in turn helped students to build bridges with workers. In short, across the board, for both worker and student, there was a key contradiction: 'the system's inability to satisfy new non-material needs which it cannot help generating'.[9]

The events of May 1968 in Paris excited Gorz as they did most radicals at the time. He saw the phenomenon as a great explosion of pent-up aspirations. The problem was that the various groups lacked the means to articulate goals which could express these basic desires and needs. All they had was the feeling that things must change.

> the form and dynamic of their action had taught them that they could obtain, and should therefore demand, *something different*, and that this 'something different' was not calculable or realizable within the framework of the system.
> 'Tell us exactly what you want,' exclaimed the bourgeois liberals to the refractory students and workers. But how were they to put it into words? The revolt itself was the only language they possessed, and it was not a language that could be translated into speeches.[10]

What was lacking, according to Gorz, was the mass revolutionary party described above. The party could have provided a language and thereby a set of goals to provide direction and continuing stimulus. The party therefore provides the desideratum of any successful revolutionary movement, for the latter 'can move forward, assert itself and bite into the existing order only if, in its progress, it evolves the outlines of a new kind of society, the instruments of its construction, functioning and future development'.[11] Without the party the element of spontaneity, vital in the right proportions, became dominant and propelled the movement to disaster.

The feeling one gets on reading these sixties pieces is of new material imprisoned in old categories. Although rejecting Bolshevik vanguardism, Gorz still reveals the heritage of Marxist-Leninist vocabulary and concepts. The working class may have changed its composition but it is still *the* revolutionary subject, the ultimate repository of revolutionary hope. The institution of the party as *the* party also reveals this link with the past. The categories are however clearly bursting at the seams. The events of May 1968 were indigestible to a Marxist-Leninist appetite, as Gorz himself was well aware. How are all these strange new social forces to be integrated? At what point do sociological changes in society destroy the status of the working class as *the* revolutionary class? What is a flexible vanguard or a mass party? Throughout, Gorz's central concern, the production of the future in the present, still shines through the opaque coating of residual Marxism-Leninism.

ENTER ECOLOGY

In the seventies an ecological dimension enters Gorz's work. He is, however, keen to distinguish his Marxist ecology from non-progressive forms. He notes that capitalism's apparently limitless ability to co-opt previously subversive ideas is borne out by the experience of the ecology movement. Capitalism initially huffed and puffed at the ecologists, correctly sensing that ecology was expensive, but then stole their clothes when it became clear that further expansion required care for the environment. Since the increased costs are passed on to others, capitalist ecology eventually leads to economic stagnation and crisis. This will not act as a springboard to revolution but merely cause social regression combined with an increase in private and public monopolies. This, Gorz argues, 'is highly probable, if capitalism is compelled to integrate ecological costs *without being challenged* at all levels by alternative social practices and an alternative vision of human civilization'.[12] Ecology itself cannot produce the alternative values and vision. Gorz uses Illich's distinction 'conviviality or technofascism'[13] to show that ecological visions can come in both liberatory and repressive forms. Nor is mere commitment to socialism in itself proof of a sound grounding – authoritarian socialism's manipulation of society and nature is profoundly reactionary. Like Bahro, Gorz finds Marxism deficient with respect to ecology. It shares the growth perspective of its capitalist opponents. As such its future perspective is, in this respect, its weakest aspect: 'Growth-oriented socialism . . . reflects the distorted image of our past, not of our future. Marxism, although irreplaceable as an instrument of analysis, has lost its prophetic value'.[14] Ecological concerns therefore have to be grounded in a visionary democratic-socialist struggle.

In *Ecology and Politics* (written c. 1974) Gorz creates something which has not really been seen since William Morris: a self-conscious Marxist utopia. Having established the principles of the new society in a theoretical preamble, he continues:

> To illustrate these theses, I shall describe one of several possible utopias. The conclusions stated above could of course be given a different expression from the one suggested here: its only function is to liberate the imagination as to the possibilities for change.[15]

The intention is, therefore, to avoid the authoritarian utopianism implicit in some types of Marxism. The model is to stimulate individual creativity in readers, not establish some kind of binding norm. It is an odd little utopia. It is very short – about eight to nine pages. The setting appears to be the day after the revolution. Although it starts with a minor literary flourish, 'When they woke up that morning, the citizens asked themselves what new turmoil awaited them',[16] this is the first and last time; thereafter it declines into that dull didactic realism so typical of the utopian genre – the stylistic range of a Morris is lacking. The central event is a television broadcast by the President and the Prime Minister where the philosophy of the revolution is expounded: 'We shall work less';[17] 'we must consume better'[18] and 'We must re-integrate culture into the everyday life of all'.[19] This is said to involve measures such as the ending of wasteful production, the creation of more durable products, educational reform, the encouragement of bicycles and small motorbikes, new work patterns, a more natural agriculture, grass-roots entertainment and, 'in order to encourage the exercise of the imagination and the greater exchange of ideas, no television programs would be broadcast on Fridays and Saturdays'.[20] This exotic last suggestion conveys something of the uncomfortable mix of authoritarian/centralist and libertarian/pluralist phenomena in Gorz's utopia. Words like 'compulsory', 'required', 'expected', 'should' and 'must' abound. They are uttered by the above-mentioned leaders in the form of dictats. On the other hand, we are told about independently-established communes and co-operatives and of the leaders themselves proclaiming that 'The government's vocation is to abdicate into the hands of the people'.[21] Gorz can be applauded for anticipating the objective contradictions that are likely to beset the new society. Since he is portraying the comparatively near future – the transitional stage of socialism and not the far distance of communism – this realistic baring of stresses and strains is all to the good. Thus, whatever one's views on the particulars of Gorz's vision, the fact that he has attempted to spell it out should be appreciated. He has moved from recognizing the necessity of utopianism to actually practising it.

ADIEUX AU PROLETARIAT

In *Farewell to the Working Class* (1980), Gorz deploys his most provocative ideas. Its central concern is 'the liberation of time and the abolition of work'.[22] 'Work' is distinguished from 'self-determined activity'. Work emerged with capitalism; it is activity undertaken for wages and for another's purposes. It is neither free nor an end in itself. It is, in short, an imposition. Self-determined activity, by contrast, is freely chosen activity, undertaken for its own sake and for one's own freely determined goals. The abolition of work is not an abstract goal – capitalism is itself actively destroying it. Increasing automation is ever lengthening the dole queues and the social structure of advanced capitalism is becoming one where there is a growing mass of unemployed, an aristocracy of skilled and tenured workers and 'a proletariat of temporary workers carrying out the least skilled and most unpleasant types of work'.[23] Members of the aristocracy of labour are implacable opponents of the abolition of work. They identify with their work because of the perceived benefits it brings them and rightly see automation as a dagger at their throat:

> Automation will always be perceived by skilled workers as a direct attack on their class insofar as it undermines workers' class power over production and eliminates the possibility to identify with one's work (or even to identify one's work at all). Thus their major concern will be to resist automation, rather than to turn its weapons against their attackers. Protecting jobs and skills, rather than seeking to control and benefit from the way in which work is abolished, will remain the major concern of traditional trade unionism.[24]

That is why they are bound to remain on the defensive.

The way forward lies with those who no longer identify with their work, who no longer see their wage labour as fulfilling and valuable in itself. Such individuals, Gorz stresses, are not unrepresentative minorities but rather, at least potentially, the vast bulk of the working population:

> All those who are 'allergic to work', as Rousselet has put it, can no longer be considered to be marginals. They are not part of a subculture existing on the fringes of society, but represent a real or potential majority of those in 'active employment' who see 'their' work as a tedious necessity in which it is impossible to be fully involved.[25]

This development is attributed by Gorz to changes in the cultural climate and to his old theme of the simultaneous intellectualizing and proletarianizing of work patterns. He terms this new social force 'a non-class of non-workers'.[26] This 'non-class', although not yet ready and able to move to the new society, none the less holds the key to that society:

> Its goal is the abolition of workers and work rather than their appropriation. And this prefigures the future world. The abolition of work can have no other social subject than this non-class. I do not infer from this that is is already capable of taking the process of abolishing work under its control and of producing a society based upon the liberation of time. All I am asserting is that such a society cannot be produced

without, or in opposition to, this non-class, but only by it or with its support.[27]

Anticipating the objection from some Marxists that a non-class cannot seize power whereas the working class can, he responds that there is no evidence that the working class can and that the notion of seizing power is itself obsolete: power should be 'dismantled, controlled, if not abolished altogether'.[28] This is developed into a general attack on the Marxist notion of the revolutionary working class which decisively breaks with the conceptions he was still willing to entertain in the sixties. The old Marxist conception of the revolutionary proletariat is now condemned as 'theological': 'The working class defined by Marx or Marxists derives its theological character from being perceived as a subject transcending its members. It makes history and builds society through the agency of its unwitting members, whatever their intentions'.[29] The non-class is quite different. It is in no way a mystical social subject: 'It has no transcendent unity or mission, and hence no overall conception of history and society. It has . . . no reality other than that of the people who compose it'.[30] It is a much more mundane but, by its reality, infinitely superior conception to the pious fictions of the past. As to the actual political form this transformation will take, Gorz displays an open-mindedness at variance with his sixties pronouncements: 'I do not know what form this action will take, or which political force might be able to take it'.[31] However, as in the sixties, he wishes to see spontaneity allied with organization.

If in the sixties Gorz was still in the grip of old Marxist-Leninist categories, his liberation seems to have produced something of a backlash against Marx and Marxism. Overstatement and error has sometimes resulted. The claim that Marxism has been robbed of prophetic value is clearly false – and belied by Gorz's own use of Marx's imagery of communism. Similarly, whereas it is undoubtedly true that Hegel's subject/object dialectic did exercise a not entirely healthy influence on Marx, the claim that Marx held a theological conception of the proletariat is untrue. Like Gorz, Marx thought it imperative that revolution spring from the experiences of actual people and he had clear sociological, not theological, reasons for his perspective on the proletariat. There does appear to be some conflation of Marxism and Marxism-Leninism in Gorz's mind.

LES CHEMINS DU PARADIS

And so we return to *Paths to Paradise*. The reference to Marxism's loss of its prophetic value is not repeated in this text which frequently returns to Marx's *Grundrisse* for Gorz's anatomy of communist society. The work naturally builds upon the succeeding texts. For Gorz, the old order is destroying itself, but it is not about to yield the promised land automatically. Many options exist and the left must create its alternative as a necessary part of the authentic transition:

> Times of crisis are also times of great freedom. Our world is out of joint; societies are distintegrating, our lifelong hopes and values are crumbling. The future ceases to be a continuation of past trends. The meaning of present development is confused; the meaning of history suspended.
>
> Because the curtain has fallen on the older order and no other order waits in the wings, we must improvise the future as never before.[32]

This does not involve a piece of arbitrary and abstract invention. Capitalism is itself creating possibilities for use in the new world. Gorz places most hope on the potential of the micro-technology revolution. Unlike some ecologically-inclined individuals, Gorz distinguishes between technologies which are inherently oppressive and those which, under the right social conditions, can promote liberation:

> Unlike the mega-technologies of the industrial era, which were an obstacle to decentralised, community-based development, automation is socially ambivalent. The mega-technologies were a one-way street, whereas micro-electronics is a crossroads: it neither excludes nor imposes a form of development.[33]

Automation will provide the backbone to society, producing for basic needs and releasing much human time for a whole range of individually chosen purposes. Throughout, he stresses the inevitable remaining dualisms of central/local, autonomy/heteronomy, freedom/necessity. Everyone, he argues, will have three levels of activity:

> 1) Heteronomous, macro-social work, organised across society as a whole, enabling it to function and providing for basic needs;

2) Micro-social activity, self-organised on a local level and based on voluntary participation, except where it replaces macro-social work in providing for basic needs;
3) Autonomous activity which corresponds to the particular desires and projects of individuals, families and small groups.[34]

This, he believes, would be true communism – the essence of Marx's most advanced vision.

Gorz's work is a valuable resource for those interested in a utopian Marxism. His assertion that utopians are the realists in our society cannot be repeated too often. Coming as it does from one who has always had a sharp eye for the realities of advanced capitalist society, it is particularly valuable. He has also sat down and constructed his own vision of future society – something which can only be to the good. His alternative may appear flawed or repugnant to some, but it is at least there and can in turn stimulate others to adopt, amend or replace it. Although critical of parts of the Marxist tradition and of Marx's own work, Gorz has still grounded his radical project in that tradition – to a much greater extent than has Bahro. His long, hard look at modern society – and at Marx – has not been the launching pad for a trajectory out of Marxism.

CONCLUSION: MARXISM AND UTOPIANISM

The distinction between utopian and scientific socialism has, on balance, been an unfortunate one for the Marxist tradition.[1] Marx and Engels initially deployed the term 'utopian socialism' for two specific reasons: they wished to highlight the distinctiveness of their own method and safeguard the fledgling communist movement from alternative political currents. With respect to the first of these there was both distortion and lack of candour. As we saw, the 'utopian socialists': Saint-Simon, Owen and Fourier, were convinced of the scientific nature of their projects and developed sophisticated analyses of their respective societies. These theories exercised great and lasting influence over Marx and Engels – an influence they only partially acknowledged. However, Marx and Engels' main targets were not these great 'utopian' thinkers, but their disciples. The bitterest remarks of Marx and Engels on 'utopian socialism' invariably occurred when they felt a political threat from these followers. Whatever their views on 'utopian socialism', Marx and Engels clearly did not rule out anticipation and freely engaged in it themselves. Neither, at his best, subscribed to the idea of the proletarian as a blind automaton, driven by supposed iron laws of history – the revolution required a consciously critical and anticipatory subject. In their role of socialist intellectuals Marx and Engels developed visions of future society, which they saw as both flowing from and consolidating the lived experience of the proletariat. Many of the details of these visions reflect again the influence of Saint-Simon, Owen and Fourier. They did, however, want to avoid foreclosing the future with images that might undermine the creative autonomy of the proletariat. The ambiguities of Marx and Engels' position proved fertile soil for their immediate successors. 'Utopianism' became a term of political abuse and a source of guilt. In the grip of a highly positivist conception of science, these Second International thinkers used 'utopian' as a medieval pontiff would use 'heresy' – it was the mark of delusion. Since this science was lifeless, utopianism had to be readmitted, but only through the back door. The two main victors from the collapse of the Second International, social democracy and communism, both worked with a distinctive, and flawed, type of utopianism. Other groups and individuals in this period grounded, and therefore to some extent disguised, their utopianism in the 'primitive' stages of society and the individual. In the twentieth century a number of thinkers have sought to develop a self-consciously utopian Marxism, recognizing the necessary benefit of the utopian dimension. Although Bloch, Marcuse, Bahro and Gorz differ greatly among themselves, they share the perspective that a Marxism without a future orientation is blind.

How then is utopianism to issue forth politically? In the introduction we spoke of a 'utopian impulse' lying at the base not only of the more familiar utopian blueprints, the utopias proper, but also of phenomena such as political ideologies, architecture, fashion and the like. In the chapters on the four twentieth century thinkers we saw various formulations of the same basic point. Amongst the strategies suggested for harnessing all this utopianism, Marxism-Leninism has proved to be the most unsatisfactory. The historical experience of Marxist-Leninist vanguards has shown a strong tendency towards authoritarian utopianism – the formulation by party élites of *one* and *only one* vision of the future. This has involved disregarding the aspirations of most ordinary people. Sheila Rowbotham has described her own experience of these vanguardists:

A sure sign of a leader of a Leninist political group is a tendency to look past your eyes and over your head when they talk to you. Either they are taking a long objective view which does not involve encountering you, or they are looking for more prestigious 'contacts' in the shape of a shop steward or so.[2]

In this respect, Marxists would do well to attend to the despised traditions of liberalism and anarchism. Liberal theory, if not always its practice, has been hostile to the implied infallibility involved in political claims to exclusive truth. The pluralist approach that has inevitably flowed from this position is enshrined in the principle that individuals are the best judges of their own interests, no matter how wrong they appear to others. Milton, a person who actually did believe in something called 'the truth', none the less warned, in the midst of the English Revolution, of the ultimate futility of mindless orthodoxy: 'A man may be a heretic in the truth; and if he believes things only because his pastor says so, or the assembly so determines, without knowing other reason, though his belief be true, yet the very truth he holds becomes his heresy . . .'.[3] If Soviet societies have confirmed Milton's worst fears, the contemptuous disregard of western vanguardist parties for alternative positions, or for so-called 'false consciousness', suggests the same mind-set. In the case of anarchism there is a proud record of putting the anti-authoritarian case in a radical context. From Proudhon's letter to Marx: 'let us give the world an example of learned and far-sighted tolerance . . . let us not pose as the apostles of a new religion',[4] via Bakunin's attack on 'these learned men and tutors of humanity'[5] and Emma Goldman ('The central authorities attempted to force the activities of the people into forms corresponding with the purposes of the party')[6] to the present day, anarchists have held aloft the banner of radical pluralism. This is not to say that it is absolutely impossible for a vanguardist party genuinely to channel popular aspirations. It requires, however, a principled commitment to – and not merely a tactical use of – democratic pluralism.

A number of interesting ideas have emerged from currents of French thought associated with Deleuze, Guattari, Foucault and Hocquenghem. Greatly influenced by the events of May 1968 in France, they stress the power and importance of what Guattari terms 'molecular revolution' – social change propelled by a whole series of superficially marginal and peripheral groups:

> Movements that elude the dominant means of identification, that produce their own referential axes, that are interlinked by their own underground and transversal connections, and consequently undermine traditional production relations, traditional social and family systems, traditional attitudes to the body, to sex, to the universe.[7]

This involves the rejection of any vanguardist strategy, the rejection of 'the indignity of speaking for others':[8]

> What is important is not an authoritarian unification, but a kind of infinite swarming of desiring machines – in schools, factories, neighbourhoods, in day nurseries, in prisons, everywhere. It is not a question of trimming or totalizing all these various partial movements, but of connecting them together on the one stem.[9]

Guy Hocquenghem, in *Homosexual Desire*, develops this strategy from a perspective of the modern gay movement – 'Homosexual action, not action in favour of homosexuality'.[10]

It is not surprising that appealing models have emerged from the modern feminist movement. Feminism has displayed a rich and creative dimension of utopianism. The classic utopia has been seen as a most appropriate form for articulating the criticisms and aspirations of women. Sarah Scott's *A Description of Millenium Hall* (1762)[11] describes a 'female Arcadia' where a number of women, after having variously endured the hazards of poverty, seduction, loveless marriages and suchlike, live on the basis of Christian morality and community of property. In Carol Farley Kessler's anthology, *Daring To Dream*,[12] we can read the utopian stories of American women in the nineteenth and early twentieth centuries with their recurring themes: the need for female education, for financial independence, for marriage reform, for the removal of domestic drudgery, for genuine recognition, for the abolition of false female roles and of the view of women as mere adjuncts of men. These are seen not as sectional demands but as women's contribution to the general enrichment of civilization. This notion of women as the bearers of values lost, rejected or distorted by male society lies at the heart of Charlotte Perkins Gilman's *Herland*[13] (1915), a socialist-feminist novel about an all-women utopia. It was, however, in the nineteen seventies that a real explosion of feminist utopias occurred, of which the best known are Marge Piercy's *Woman On The Edge Of Time*[14] and Ursula LeGuin's *The Dispossessed*.[15] As Rohrlich and Baruch show, in their fascinating collection *Women in Search of Utopia*,[16] women throughout history have both developed and joined utopian social forms in tune with their deepest aspirations, such as the medieval

Beguines, the Shakers, the Spanish anarchists, Findhorn in Scotland and the Peace Camps. Along with the utopianism displayed in a whole host of other spheres has come a sharp critique of traditional socialism – an awareness of the lacunae in the goals and of the discrepancy between ends and means. Radical women directly experienced the authoritarian utopianism of the traditional left. Women's liberation, if mentioned at all, was to be some kind of mysterious by-product of the party-led revolution. The ethos and organizational form of these parties inhibited or repelled women. *Beyond the Fragments*, by Sheila Rowbotham, Lynne Segal and Hilary Wainwright, brings to bear on the question of socialist organization insights drawn from the experience of feminists. The authors advocate a growing unity of autonomous groups, building upon *ad hoc* alliances. Each group – be it a women's group, tenants' associations etc. – develops its own vision and refines and amends this in contact with other groups: no external body of professional revolutionaries watches over and guides along the right line. Hilary Wainwright uses the analogy of weaving:

> In effect left-wing trades councils, socialist resource centres, socialist women's groups, theatre groups, left bookshops, militant shop stewards' committees . . . carry out, in sum, the functions of a socialist party but without the coordination and long term perspective of a party. It is as if the different parts of a piece of cloth – a political organization – were being woven creatively and with *ad hoc* contact between the weavers, but without anyone having a master plan. Though occasionally we need, from different points, to stand back and see where we've got to, where the cloth is weak and where the pattern is becoming blurred.[17]

There is an attractive open-endedness to this conception. If one wanted to make a criticism it would be in terms of a residual old-leftism. The definition of progressive forces is perhaps too restrictive. When the left first encountered the women's movement, as we have already said, it tended to reject the movement's claims, feeling that such developments posed a serious threat to its working-class orientation. When the movement, and other groups such as gays, didn't go away, the left was forced to rejig its theory – but it never quite worked. The new elements were rather uncomfortably tacked on. Hilary Wainwright's conception is to an extent doing the same, but from the other pole – the old idea of the working class revolution is tacked on to the concept of the autonomous movements.

It is not helpful to think in terms of a sharp dualism – autonomous movements *or* democratic parties. The problems with vanguardist parties have already been discussed, but, as stated then, this in no way rules out the use of party (especially of other types) as a channel for utopian aspirations. In Britain, for example, a strategy involving the Labour Party *and* myriad micro movements is quite conceivable. The obvious problems with the relationships between movements and parties are by no means insuperable. A party should be seen as merely one forum amongst many, possessing like any other its own advantages and weaknesses.

Modern society is constantly creating new desires and reinforcing old needs. Some of these are in its own repressive interests, but many it cannot satisfy in its present form. In countless ways, people are demonstrating their dissatisfaction with the existing world and their dream of something better. What is required is a strategy which is sensitive to these aspirations in all social classes. Individual groups campaigning on specific issues should not merely seek the assistance of other overtly socialist individuals and groups but should recognize potential allies in the unlikeliest of areas. Only in this way will they tune into the real movement for change in modern society. Short-sighted and narrow purism is a recipe for stagnation.

At the end of the last century, Oscar Wilde recognized the centrality of utopia for human progress:

> A map of the world which does not include Utopia is not worth glancing at, for it leaves out the one country at which Humanity is always landing. And when Humanity lands there, it looks out and, seeing a better country, sets sail. Progress is the realisation of Utopias.[18]

Mind you, four years later he was in jail.

NOTES

INTRODUCTION: IN PRAISE OF UTOPIANISM

1 Useful discussions of the concept can be found in: S. Rowbotham, 'Hopes, dreams & dirty nappies', *Marxism Today*, December 1984, 8–12; L. Kolakowski, 'The death of utopia reconsidered', in S. McMurrin (ed.), *The Tanner Lectures on Human Values IV*, Cambridge: Cambridge University Press 1983, 229–47; H. J. N. Horsburgh, 'The relevance of the utopian', *Ethics*, LXVII, October 1956, 127–38; T. Kenyon, 'Utopia in reality: "Ideal" societies in social and political theory', *History of Political Thought*, III (1), January 1982, 123–55; B. Goodwin and K. Taylor, *The Politics of Utopia*, London: Hutchinson 1982. For a history of utopian thought see F. E. Manuel and F. P. Manuel, *Utopian Thought in the Western World*, Oxford: Basil Blackwell 1979. A very recent addition to the literature is K. Kumar, *Utopia and Anti-Utopia in Modern Times*, Oxford: Basil Blackwell 1987.
2 T. More, *Utopia*, Harmondsworth: Penguin 1965, 128–31.
3 N. Machiavelli, *The Prince*, Harmondsworth: Penguin 1961, 90–91.
4 For Bloch see chapter six; also K. Mannheim, *Ideology and Utopia*, London: Routledge & Kegan Paul 1936.
5 S. Freud, *Art and Literature*, Harmondsworth: Penguin 1985, 134.
6 J. L. Singer, *Daydreaming and Fantasy*, Oxford: Oxford University Press 1981, 72.
7 Freud, *Art and Literature*, 134.
8 Singer, *Daydreaming and Fantasy*, chapter three.
9 Freud, *Art and Literature*, 133.
10 J. Thurber, *Vintage Thurber*, Harmondsworth: Penguin 1983, 27–30.
11 K. Waterhouse, *Billy Liar*, Harmondsworth: Penguin 1962, 5.
12 B. Anderson, *Imagined Communities*, London: Verso 1983.
13 A useful recent article on this subject is R. Levitas, 'New right utopias', *Radical Philosophy*, 39, Spring 1985, 2–9.
14 E. Hobsbawm and T. Ranger, *The Invention of Tradition*, Cambridge: Cambridge University Press 1983.

15 R. Fishman, 'Utopia in three dimensions: the ideal city and the origins of modern design', in P. Alexander and R. Gill, *Utopias*, London: Duckworth 1984, 95–107.
16 C. Dickens, *Great Expectations*, Harmondsworth: Penguin 1965, 87.
17 E. O'Neill, *Long Day's Journey into Night*, London: Jonathan Cape 1966, 100.
18 E. Wilson, *Adorned in Dreams*, London: Virago 1985, 246–7.
19 H. M. Enzenberger, 'Constituents of a theory of the media', *New Left Review*, 64, 1970, 24–5.
20 Mannheim, *Ideology and Utopia*, 176–7.
21 K. Popper, *Conjectures and Refutations*, London: Routledge & Kegan Paul 1972, chapter eighteen.
22 M. Oakeshott, *Rationalism in Politics*, London: Methuen 1967.

1 THE UTOPIAN SOCIALISTS

1 The standard biography of Saint-Simon is: F. E. Manuel, *The New World of Henri Saint-Simon*, Notre Dame: University of Notre Dame 1963. Saint-Simon and the other main utopian socialists are considered in K. Taylor, *The Political Ideas of the Utopian Socialists*, London: Frank Cass 1982. Two translated selections of Saint-Simon's writings worth consulting are G. Ionescu (ed.), *The Political Thought of Saint-Simon*, Oxford: Oxford University Press 1976, and K. Taylor (trans. and ed.), *Henri Saint-Simon: Selected Writings on Science, Industry and Social Organisation*, London: Croom Helm 1975.
2 Ionescu, *The Political Thought of Saint-Simon*, 160.
3 T. Paine, *Rights of Man*, Harmondsworth: Penguin 1969, 107.
4 Manuel, *The New World of Henri Saint-Simon*, 200–1.
5 Taylor, *Henri Saint-Simon Selected Writings on Science, Industry and Social Organisation*, 209.
6 ibid., 209.
7 Ionescu, *The Political Thought of Saint-Simon*, 228.
8 For Owen see J. F. C. Harrison, *Robert Owen and the Owenites in Britain and America: The Quest for the New Moral World*, London: Routledge & Kegan Paul 1969. A useful selection of his work can be found in A. L. Morton (ed.), *The Life and Ideas of Robert Owen*, London: Lawrence and Wishart 1968.
9 R. Owen, *The Life of Robert Owen*, I, London: Frank Cass 1967, 271.
10 ibid., 117.
11 ibid., 104.
12 ibid., 265.
13 ibid., xxxi–xxxii.
14 E. P. Thompson, *The Making of the English Working Class*, Harmondsworth: Penguin 1980, 884.
15 B. Taylor, *Eve and the New Jerusalem*, London: Virago 1983.
16 Quoted in J. Karabel, 'The failure of American socialism reconsidered', *The Socialist Register 1979*, London: Merlin 1979, 207.

17 Owen, *The Life of Robert Owen*, xviii.
18 ibid., xxx–xxxi.
19 For Fourier see M. C. Spencer, *Charles Fourier*, Boston: Twayne 1981; collections of his writings include: J. Beecher and R. Bienvenu, *The Utopian Vision of Charles Fourier*, London: Jonathan Cape 1975; F. E. Manuel, *Design for Utopia*, New York: Schocken 1971; M. Poster, *Harmonian Man*, New York: Doubleday 1971.
20 Beecher and Bienvenu, *The Utopian Vision of Charles Fourier*, 82.
21 Quoted in Spencer, *Charles Fourier*, 126.
22 Beecher and Bienvenu, *The Utopian Vision of Charles Fourier*, 155.
23 ibid., 113.
24 ibid., 93.
25 Manuel, *Design for Utopia*, 55.
26 R. Barthes, *Sade Fourier Loyola*, London: Jonathan Cape 1977, 87.
27 Beecher and Bienvenu, *The Utopian Vision of Charles Fourier*, 99.
28 ibid., 215.
29 Quoted in Barthes, *Sade Fourier Loyola*, 86.
30 Beecher and Bienvenu, *The Utopian Vision of Charles Fourier*, 87.
31 C. Gide, 'Introduction' to Manuel, *Design for Utopia*, 21.
32 Beecher and Bienvenu, *The Utopian Vision of Charles Fourier*, 354.
33 ibid., 196.
34 Manuel, *Design for Utopia*, 14.
35 A. Breton, *What is Surrealism?*, London: Pluto 1978, 192.
36 ibid., 250.
37 Beecher and Bienvenu, *The Utopian Vision of Charles Fourier*, 200.

2 MARX, ENGELS AND UTOPIANISM

1 K. Marx and F. Engels, *Collected Works*, London: Lawrence & Wishart 1975, 3, 394.
2 ibid., 394.
3 ibid., 394.
4 Marx and Engels, *Collected Works*, 4, 252.
5 ibid., 214.
6 Marx and Engels, *Collected Works*, 3, 400.
7 Marx and Engels, *Collected Works*, 4, 253.
8 Marx and Engels, *Collected Works*, 38, 25.
9 ibid., 26.
10 ibid., 27.
11 G. Gurvitch, 'La sociologie du jeune Marx', *Cahiers Internationaux De Sociologie*, III, pt 4, 1948.
12 W. Blumenberg, *Karl Marx*, London: New Left Books 1972, 44–6.
13 T. Bottomore, *Karl Marx*, Oxford: Basil Blackwell 1973, 5.
14 Blumenberg, *Karl Marx*, 44–5.
15 Gurvitch, 'La sociologie du jeune Marx', 14.
16 Marx and Engels, *Collected Works*, 3, 30.
17 D. Ryazanoff (ed.), *The Communist Manifesto*, London: Martin Lawrence 1930, 232.

18 ibid., 234.
19 S. Avineri, *The Social and Political Thought of Karl Marx*, Cambridge: Cambridge University Press 1968, 53–5.
20 Marx and Engels, *Collected Works*, 3, 355.
21 ibid., 355.
22 ibid., 201.
23 Marx and Engels, *Collected Works*, 4, 196.
24 ibid., 88.
25 V. I. Lenin, *Collected Works*, London: Lawrence & Wishart 1963, 19, 23–4.
26 Marx and Engels, *Collected Works*, 5, 461.
27 ibid., 462.
28 ibid., 462.
29 Marx and Engels, *Collected Works*, 4, 525.
30 Quoted in D. McLellan, *Karl Marx: His Life and Thought*, London: Macmillan 1973, 156–7.
31 Quoted in R. Plant *Hegel*, London: Allen & Unwin 1973, 83.
32 G. Hegel, *Phenomenology of Spirit*, Oxford: Oxford University Press 1979, 151. This passage is discussed in E. Sherover-Marcuse, *Emancipation and Consciousness*, Oxford: Basil Blackwell 1986, 108–9.
33 Marx and Engels, *Collected Works*, 6, 515.
34 ibid., 516.
35 ibid., 516.
36 K. Marx and F. Engels, *Selected Correspondence*, Moscow: Progress 1975, 172.
37 K. Marx and F. Engels, *On the Paris Commune*, Moscow: Progress 1980, 166.
38 ibid., 76. The different versions are discussed in an interesting section of M. J. Lasky, *Utopia and Revolution*, Chicago: Chicago University Press 1976, 36–43.
39 K. Marx and F. Engels, *Selected Works*, London: Lawrence & Wishart 1970, 246.
40 F. Engels, *Socialism: Utopian and Scientific*, Peking: Foreign Languages Press 1975, 7–8.
41 H. Marcuse, *Reason and Revolution*, London: Routledge & Kegan Paul 1968, 318.
42 Marx and Engels, *Collected Works*, 6, 515.
43 K. Marx, *The First International and After*, Harmondsworth: Penguin 1974, 82.
44 Marx and Engels, *Collected Works*, 5, 49.
45 Marx and Engels, *Selected Works*, 508.
46 Marx and Engels, *Selected Correspondence*, 318.
47 ibid., 318.
48 ibid., 318.
49 K. Marx and F. Engels, *The Communist Manifesto*, Harmondsworth: Penguin 1967, 53–4.
50 ibid., 54.
51 Engels, *Socialism: Utopian and Scientific*, 54.
52 F. Engels, *Anti-Dühring*, London: Lawrence & Wishart 1975, 348.

53 D. McLellan, *Marx's Grundrisse*, London: Granada 1971, 146.
54 B. Ollman, 'Marx's vision of communism: a reconstruction', *Critique*, 8, Summer 1977, 7.

3 THE SECOND INTERNATIONAL

1 Quoted in M. Salvadori, *Karl Kautsky and the Socialist Revolution 1880–1938*, London: New Left Books 1979, 66.
2 K. Kautsky, *Thomas More and His Utopia*, London: Lawrence & Wishart 1979, 161.
3 Salvadori, *Karl Kautsky*, 76.
4 V. I. Lenin, *Collected Works*, London: Lawrence & Wishart 1961, 5, 383–4.
5 Salvadori, *Karl Kautsky*, 76.
6 K. Kautsky, *The Social Revolution*, Chicago: Kerr & Co. 1916, 103–4.
7 K. Marx and F. Engels, *Collected Works*, London: Lawrence & Wishart 1975, 5, 4.
8 J. P. Nettl, 'The German Social Democratic Party, 1890–1914, as a political model', *Past and Present*, 30, 1965, 73.
9 D. W. Lovell, *From Marx to Lenin*, Cambridge: Cambridge University Press 1984, 92.
10 ibid., 92.
11 K. Kautsky, *The Social Revolution*, 104.
12 See S. B. Knoll, 'Socialism as dystopia: political uses of utopian dime novels in pre World War I Germany', in E. D. Wilson (ed.), *Society For Utopian Studies: Eighth Annual Conference*, Indiana, PA: Society for Utopian Studies 1984.
13 L. Kolakowski, *Main Currents of Marxism: The Golden Age*, Oxford: Oxford University Press 1978, 47.
14 D. Kellner (ed.), *Karl Korsch: Revolutionary Theory*, Austin: University of Texas Press 1977, 127.
15 ibid., 127–8.
16 ibid., 127.
17 Quoted in M. J. Lasky, *Utopia and Revolution*, Chicago: Chicago University Press 1976, 105.
18 E. Bernstein, *Evolutionary Socialism*, New York: Schocken 1961, 210.
19 ibid., 210–11.
20 ibid., xxix.
21 ibid., xxix.
22 L. Trotsky, *Political Profiles*, London: New Park 1972, 66.
23 Bernstein, *Evolutionary Socialism*, 212.
24 D. Howard (ed.), *Selected Political Writings of Rosa Luxemburg*, New York: Monthly Review Press 1971, 53.
25 ibid., 53.
26 ibid., 245.
27 ibid., 306.
28 R. Luxemburg, *Comrade and Lover*, London: Pluto 1979, 8.
29 ibid., 152–3.

30 K. Hunt, 'Crossing the river of fire: the socialist construction of women's politicization', in J. Evans *et al.* *Feminism and Political Theory*, London: Sage 1986, 60–61; see also R. Dunayevskaya, *Rosa Luxemburg, Women's Liberation, and Marx's Philosophy of Revolution*, Brighton: Harvester 1982.
31 Howard, *Selected Political Writings of Rosa Luxemburg*, 60.
32 P. Goode (ed.), *Karl Kautsky: Selected Political Writings*, London: Macmillan 1983, 133.
33 Bernstein, *Evolutionary Socialism*, 219.
34 E. Bernstein, *Cromwell and Communism*, Nottingham: Spokesman 1980.
35 K. Marx and F. Engels, *The Communist Manifesto*, Harmondsworth: Penguin 1967, 56. K. Marx and F. Engels, *Selected Correspondence*, Moscow: Progress 1975, 319–20.
36 G. Plekhanov, *Selected Philosophical Works*, Moscow: Progress 1977, 1, 537–8.
37 ibid., 531.
38 ibid., 361.
39 ibid., 359.
40 ibid., 128.
41 N. Harding and R. Taylor, *Marxism in Russia: Key Documents 1879–1906*, Cambridge: Cambridge University Press 1983, 251.
42 ibid., 251.
43 ibid., 253.
44 ibid., 244.
45 Plekhanov, *Selected Philosophical Works*, 2, 372.
46 Lenin, *Collected Works*, 5, 375.
47 ibid., 509–10.
48 Lenin, *Collected Works*, 38, 373.
49 W. F. Woehrlin, *Chernyshevskii: The Man and the Journalist*, Cambridge: Harvard University Press 1971, 186.
50 N. Chernyshevsky, *What is to be Done?*, London: Virago 1982, 72.
51 Lenin, *Collected Works*, 14, 361.
52 Lenin, *Collected Works*, 31, 71.
53 Lenin, *Collected Works*, 25, 425.
54 Lenin, *Collected Works*, 18, 355.
55 ibid., 359.
56 Lenin, *Collected Works*, 25, 384.

4 GOLDEN AGES AND MYTHS

1 K. Marx and F. Engels, *Selected Works*, London: Lawrence & Wishart 1970, 96.
2 ibid., 97.
3 ibid., 97.
4 ibid., 98.
5 K. Marx and F. Engels, *Collected Works*, London: Lawrence & Wishart 1977, 3, 177.

6 Marx and Engels, *Selected Works*, 449.
7 ibid., 519.
8 ibid., 583.
9 K. Marx and F. Engels, *Selected Correspondence*, Moscow: Progress 1975, 347.
10 ibid., 351.
11 P. Lafargue, *The Right To Be Lazy*, Chicago: Charles H. Kerr n.d., 32.
12 ibid., 29.
13 F. Engels, P. and L. Lafargue, *Correspondence: Volume 1 1868–1886*, Moscow: Foreign Languages Publishing House 1959, 206.
14 ibid., 298.
15 P. Lafargue, *The Evolution of Property from Savagery to Civilization*, London: Swann Sonnenschein 1890, 8.
16 ibid., 173.
17 H.-J. Steinberg, 'Workers' libraries in Germany before 1914', *History Workshop*, 1, 1976, 174.
18 A. Bebel, *Women Under Socialism*, New York: Schocken 1971, 347–49.
19 W. Reich, *Sex-Pol Essays, 1929–1934*, New York: Vintage 1972, 103.
20 ibid., 248.
21 J. Strachey, *The Theory and Practice of Socialism*, London: Gollanz 1936, 194.
22 A. L. Morton (ed.), *Political Writings of William Morris*, London: Lawrence & Wishart 1973, 189. For Morris see: P. Meier, *William Morris: The Marxist Dreamer*, Hassocks: The Harvester Press 1978, two volumes; E. P. Thompson, *William Morris: Romantic to Revolutionary*, London: Merlin 1977; other selections of Morris' work include: Asa Briggs (ed.), *William Morris: News from Nowhere and Selected Writings and Designs*, Harmondsworth: Penguin 1984; A. L. Morton (ed.), *Three Works by William Morris*, London: Lawrence & Wishart 1973.
23 Briggs, *William Morris: News from Nowhere and Selected Writings and Designs*, 159–60.
24 M. Morris, *William Morris: Artist Writer Socialist*, Oxford: Basil Blackwell 1936, 1, 292.
25 ibid., 285.
26 ibid., 283.
27 ibid., 282.
28 ibid., 289.
29 W. Morris, 'The development of modern society', *The Commonweal*, August 16, 1890, 261.
30 M. Morris, *William Morris: Artist Writer Socialist*, 2, 506.
31 K. O. Morgan, *Keir Hardie: Radical Socialist*, London: Wiedenfeld & Nicolson 1975, 206.
32 Quoted in D. Howell, *British Workers and the Independent Labour Party 1888–1906*, Manchester: Manchester University Press 1983, 355.
33 ibid., 354–5.
34 P. B. Ellis (ed.), *James Connolly: Selected Writings*, Harmondsworth: Penguin 1973, 124. For Connolly see: C. D. Greaves, *The Life and*

Times of James Connolly, London: Lawrence & Wishart 1976; B. Ransom, *Connolly's Marxism*, London: Pluto 1980; another selection of Connolly's writings can be found in O. D. Edwards and B. Ransom (eds), *James Connolly: Selected Political Writings*, London: Jonathan Cape 1973.

35 Edwards and Ransom, *James Connolly: Selected Political Writings*, 173.
36 J. Connolly, *Labour in Irish History*, Dublin: New Books Publications 1971, xxxii.
37 Greaves, *The Life and Times of James Connolly*, 177.
38 Edwards and Ransom, *James Connolly: Selected Political Writings*, 173.
39 ibid., 174.
40 P. B. Ellis, *A History of the Irish Working Class*, London: Pluto 1985, 13.
41 Quoted in C. Frayling and R. Snowdon, 'Perspectives on craft', *Crafts*, January/February 1982, 17.
42 J. L. Stanley (ed.), *From Georges Sorel: Essays in Socialism and Philosophy*, New York: Oxford University Press 1976, 150. For Sorel see: J. R. Jennings, *Georges Sorel: The Character and Development of His Thought*, Basingstoke: Macmillan/St Anthony's 1985; L. Portis, *Georges Sorel*, London: Pluto 1986.
43 Stanley, *From Georges Sorel*, 150.
44 ibid., 202.
45 ibid., 202.
46 ibid., 209.
47 ibid., 210.
48 ibid., 211–12.

5 STALINISM AND AUTHORITARIAN UTOPIANISM

1 P. Goode (ed.), *Karl Kautsky: Selected Political Writings*, London: Macmillan 1983, 133.
2 Quoted in J. Berger, *Art and Revolution: Ernst Neizvestny and the Role of the Artist in the USSR*, Harmondsworth: Penguin 1969, 39.
3 *History of the Communist Party of the Soviet Union (Bolsheviks)*, Moscow: Foreign Languages Publishing House 1939, 36–7.
4 ibid., 114–15.
5 ibid., 358.
6 Rod Hague of the University of Newcastle upon Tyne told me this joke.
7 W. Leonhard, *Child of the Revolution*, London: Collins 1957, 50–1.
8 J. Fyfe, *Lysenko is Right*, London: Lawrence & Wishart 1950.
9 M. Djilas, *Rise and Fall*, Basingstoke: Macmillan 1985, 238.
10 Quoted in D. Caute, *The Fellow Travellers*, London: Quartet 1977, 3. Another excellent study of this phenomenon is N. Wood, *Communism and British Intellectuals*, London: Gollancz 1959.
11 Caute, *The Fellow Travellers*, 9.
12 ibid., 64.

13 ibid., 67.
14 ibid., 6–7.
15 P. Seale and M. McConville, *Philby: The Long Road to Moscow*, Harmondsworth: Penguin 1978, 74.
16 K. Philby, *My Silent War*, Frogmore: Granada 1969, 17.
17 S. R. Allan, *Comrades and Citizens*, London: Gollancz 1938.
18 E. Winter, *Red Virtue*, London: Gollancz 1933.
19 W. Frank, *Dawn in Russia*, New York: C. Scribner's sons 1932.
20 S. Harper, *The Russia I Believe In*, Chicago: University of Chicago Press 1945.
21 D. Collard, *Soviet Justice and the Trial of Radek and Others*, London: Gollancz 1937.
22 S. and B. Webb, *Soviet Communism: A New Civilization*, London: Longmans 1937.
23 P. Sloan, *Soviet Democracy*, London: Gollancz 1937, 111.
24 ibid., 111.
25 ibid., 106.
26 H. Johnson, *The Socialist Sixth of the World*, London: Gollancz 1939, 119.
27 ibid., 349.
28 ibid., 355–6.
29 V. Kravchenko, *I Chose Freedom*, London: Robert Hale 1947, 472.
30 R. Crossman (ed.), *The God That Failed: Six Studies in Communism*, London: Hamish Hamilton 1950, 82.
31 D. Hyde, *I Believed: The Autobiography of a former British Communist*, London: Heinemann 1951.
32 Quoted in N. Wood, *Communism and British Intellectuals*, 200.
33 J. L. Talmon, *The Origins of Totalitarian Democracy*, London: Sphere 1970, 249.
34 ibid., 254–5.
35 See L. Schapiro, *Totalitarianism*, London: Macmillan 1972.
36 Quoted in B. Crick, *George Orwell: A Life*, Harmondsworth: Penguin 1982, 450.
37 ibid., 507.
38 ibid., 567.
39 S. Williams, *Politics is for People*, Harmondsworth: Penguin 1981, 41.
40 ibid., 32–3.

6 ERNST BLOCH AND THE UBIQUITY OF UTOPIA

1 For Bloch see W. Hudson, *The Marxist Philosophy of Ernst Bloch*, London: Macmillan 1982.
2 E. Bloch, *The Principle of Hope*, Oxford: Basil Blackwell 1986, three volumes, 7.
3 ibid., 12.
4 ibid., 26.
5 ibid., 29.
6 ibid., 32.

7 ibid., 35.
8 ibid., 41.
9 ibid., 28.
10 ibid., 31.
11 ibid., 31.
12 ibid., 56.
13 ibid., 64.
14 ibid., 59.
15 ibid., 64.
16 ibid., 66.
17 ibid., 76.
18 ibid., 116.
19 ibid., 125.
20 ibid., 339.
21 ibid., 366.
22 ibid., 369.
23 ibid., 394.
24 ibid., 394.
25 ibid., 409.
26 ibid., 445–6.
27 E. Bloch, 'Nonsynchronism and the obligation to its dialectics', *New German Critique*, 11, 1977, 22.
28 ibid., 38.
29 ibid., 27.
30 Bloch, *The Principle of Hope*, 479.
31 ibid., 496.
32 ibid., 500.
33 ibid., 595.
34 ibid., 611.
35 ibid., 813.
36 ibid., 622.
37 ibid., 947.
38 ibid., 1063.
39 M. Solomon (ed.), *Marxism and Art*, Hassocks: Harvester 1979, 584.
40 Bloch, *The Principle of Hope*, 1063.
41 ibid., 1103.
42 K. Marx and F. Engels, *On Religion*, London: Lawrence & Wishart 1958, 42.
43 ibid., 42.
44 Bloch, *The Principle of Hope*, 1199.
45 E. Bloch, *Atheism in Christianity*, New York: Herder & Herder 1972, frontispiece.
46 Bloch, *The Principle of Hope*, 595.
47 E. Bloch, 'A jubilee for renegades', *New German Critique*, 4, 1975, 18.
48 E. Bloch, *On Karl Marx*, New York: Herder & Herder 1971, 139.
49 M. Landmann, 'Talking with Ernst Bloch: Korcula, 1968', *Telos*, 25, 1975, 171.
50 Bloch, *On Karl Marx*, 169.

7 HERBERT MARCUSE TURNS TO SIGMUND FREUD

1 For Marcuse see D. Kellner, *Herbert Marcuse and the Crisis of Marxism*, Basingstoke: Macmillan 1984; B. Katz, *Herbert Marcuse and the Art of Liberation*, London: Verso 1982; V. Geoghegan, *Reason and Eros: The Social Theory of Herbert Marcuse*, London: Pluto 1981.
2 H. Marcuse, *Negations*, Harmondsworth: Penguin 1972, 154.
3 ibid., 154.
4 ibid., 154.
5 ibid., 155.
6 See the various pieces included in S. Freud, *Civilization, Society and Religion: Group Psychology, Civilization and its Discontents and other Works*, Harmondsworth: Penguin 1985.
7 ibid., 185.
8 ibid., 358.
9 ibid., 358.
10 H. Marcuse, *Eros and Civilization*, London: Sphere 1972, 110.
11 ibid., 111.
12 Quoted in B. Russell, *History of Western Philosophy*, London: George Allen & Unwin 1961, 38–9.
13 Plato, *Protagoras and Meno*, Harmondsworth: Penguin 1956, 130.
14 Plato, *The Republic*, Harmondsworth: Penguin 1955, 393–401.
15 Freud, *Civilization, Society and Religion*, 256.
16 ibid., 73.
17 Marcuse, *Eros and Civilization*, 33.
18 ibid., 108.
19 ibid., 57.
20 ibid., 65.
21 ibid., 109.
22 ibid., 33.
23 ibid., 163.
24 H. Marcuse, *One Dimensional Man*, London: Sphere 1972, 89.
25 Marcuse, *Eros and Civilization*, 163.
26 ibid., 164.
27 ibid., 143.
28 ibid., 144–5.
29 ibid., 143.
30 Marcuse, *Negations*, 118.
31 ibid., 120.
32 Marcuse, *Eros and Civilization*, 130.
33 H. Marcuse, *An Essay on Liberation*, Harmondsworth: Penguin 1972, 52.
34 H. Marcuse, *Counter-Revolution and Revolt*, London: Allen Lane 1972, 116–17.
35 H. Marcuse, *Five Lectures*, London: Allen Lane 1970, 63.
36 ibid., 63.
37 ibid., 63.
38 ibid., 63.

39 Marcuse, *An Essay on Liberation*, 30.
40 ibid., 13.

8 RUDOLF BAHRO: EAST AND WEST

1 For Bahro see: U. Wolter (ed.), *Rudolf Bahro: Critical Responses*, White Plains: M. E. Sharpe 1980; R. Williams, 'Beyond actually existing socialism', *New Left Review*, 120, March/April 1980; R. Miliband, 'A commentary on Rudolf Bahro's alternative', *The Socialist Register 1979*, London: Merlin 1979.
2 M. Vajda, *The State and Socialism*, London: Allison & Busby 1981, 78.
3 B. Agger, *Western Marxism: An Introduction: Classical and Contemporary Sources*, Santa Monica: Goodyear 1979, 217.
4 ibid., 217.
5 ibid., 219.
6 ibid., 219.
7 ibid., 208.
8 Quoted in M. D. Conway, *The Life of Thomas Paine*, London: Watts & Co. 1909, 5.
9 *Encounter*, 3, LXVI, March 1986, 38.
10 M. Haraszti, *A Worker in a Worker's State*, Harmondsworth: Penguin 1977, 144.
11 ibid., 142.
12 J.-Y. Potel, *The Summer Before the Frost*, London: Pluto 1982, 93.
13 A. Heller, *The Theory of Need in Marx*, London: Allison & Busby 1976, 130.
14 A. Hegedus, A. Heller, M. Markus and M. Vajda, *The Humanisation of Socialism: Writings of the Budapest School*, London: Allison & Busby 1976, 142.
15 H. Marcuse, 'Protosocialism and late capitalism: toward a theoretical synthesis based on Bahro's analysis', in Wolter (ed.), *Rudolf Bahro: Critical Responses*, 25.
16 R. Bahro, *The Alternative in Eastern Europe*, London: New Left Books 1978, 116.
17 ibid., 253.
18 ibid., 257.
19 ibid., 257.
20 ibid., 259.
21 ibid., 265.
22 ibid., 266.
23 ibid., 271.
24 ibid., 271.
25 ibid., 275.
26 ibid., 304.
27 ibid., 305.
28 ibid., 272–3.
29 ibid., 348.

30 ibid., 350.
31 ibid., 350.
32 R. Bahro, *From Red to Green*, London: Verso 1984, 218.
33 ibid., 218.
34 ibid., 219.
35 ibid., 220.
36 R. Bahro, *Socialism and Survival*, London: Heretic Books 1982, 13.
37 R. Bahro, *Building the Green Movement*, London: GMP 1986, 79.
38 ibid., 90.
39 F. Capra and C. Spretnak, *Green Politics: The Global Promise*, London: Hutchinson 1984, 26.
40 ibid., 27.
41 Bahro, *Building the Green Movement*, 210.
42 Bahro, *From Red to Green*, 222.
43 ibid., 211.
44 Bahro, *Building the Green Movement*, 211.

9 ANDRÉ GORZ

1 For Gorz see: A. Hirsch, *The French New Left: An Intellectual History from Sartre to Gorz*, Boston: South End Press 1981; M. Foster, *Existential Marxism in Postwar France: From Sartre to Althusser*, Princeton: Princeton University Press 1975.
2 A. Gorz, *Paths to Paradise: On the Liberation from Work*, London: Pluto 1985, vii.
3 ibid., vii.
4 A. Gorz, *Socialism and Revolution*, London: Allen Lane 1975, 80.
5 ibid., 80.
6 ibid., 176.
7 ibid., 125–6.
8 ibid., 126.
9 ibid., 17.
10 ibid., 38–9.
11 ibid., 36.
12 A. Gorz, *Ecology as Politics*, London: Pluto 1983, 7.
13 ibid., 17.
14 ibid., 11.
15 ibid., 42.
16 ibid., 42.
17 ibid., 44.
18 ibid., 45.
19 ibid., 45.
20 ibid., 50.
21 ibid., 48.
22 A. Gorz, *Farewell to the Working Class: An Essay on Post-Industrial Socialism*, London: Pluto 1982, 1.
23 ibid., 3.

24 ibid., 6–7.
25 ibid., 7.
26 ibid., 7.
27 ibid., 7.
28 ibid., 8.
29 ibid., 10.
30 ibid., 11.
31 ibid., 13.
32 Gorz, *Paths to Paradise*, 1.
33 ibid., 29.
34 ibid., 63.

CONCLUSION: MARXISM AND UTOPIANISM

1 Interesting discussions can be found in: S. Lukes, 'Marxism and utopianism', in P. Alexander and R. Gill, *Utopias*, London: Duckworth 1984, 153–167; F. Jameson, 'Introduction/Prospectus: to reconsider the relationship of Marxism to utopian thought', *The Minnesota Review*, N.S.VI, 1976, 53–8; D. Suvin, ' "Utopian" and "Scientific": two attributes for socialism from Engels', *The Minnesota Review*, N.S.VI, 1976, 59–70; M. Solomon, 'Marx and Bloch: reflection on utopia and art', *Telos*, 13, 1972, 68–85; M. Meisner, *Marxism Maoism and Utopianism*, Madison: The University of Wisconsin Press 1982, chapter 1; many of the ideas in this book can be found in an earlier paper: V. Geoghegan, 'Marxism and utopianism', in G. Beauchamp, K. Roemer and N. Smith (eds), *Utopian Studies I*, Lanham: University Press of America 1987.

2 S. Rowbotham, L. Segal and H. Wainwright, *Beyond the Fragments*, London: Merlin, 1979, 130.

3 R. Eccleshall, *British Liberalism: Liberal thought from the 1640's to 1980's*, London: Longman 1986, 68.

4 G. Woodcock (ed.), *The Anarchist Reader*, Glasgow: Fontana/Collins 1977, 139.

5 M. Bakunin, *Marxism, Freedom and the State*, London: Freedom Press 1984, 19.

6 Woodcock, *The Anarchist Reader*, 153.

7 F. Guattari, *Molecular Revolution*, Harmondsworth: Penguin 1984, 269–70.

8 G. Deleuze and M. Foucault, 'The intellectuals and power: a discussion', *Telos*, 16, 1973, 105.

9 F. Guattari, *Molecular Revolution*, 230.

10 G. Hocquenghem, *Homosexual Desire*, London: Allison & Busby 1978, 119.

11 S. Scott, *Millenium Hall*, London: Virago 1986.

12 C. F. Kessler, *Daring to Dream*, Boston: Pandora 1984.

13 C. P. Gilman, *Herland*, London: The Women's Press 1979.

14 M. Piercy, *Woman On The Edge Of Time*, London: The Women's Press 1979.
15 U. LeGuin, *The Dispossessed*, London: Grafton 1975.
16 R. Rohrlich and E. H. Baruch, *Women in Search of Utopia: Mavericks and Mythmakers*, New York: Schocken 1984.
17 Rowbotham, Segal and Wainwright, *Beyond The Fragments*, 224–5.
18 O. Wilde, *Plays, Prose Writings and Poems*, London: Dent 1930, 270.

SELECT BIBLIOGRAPHY

Agger, B. (1979) *Western Marxism: An Introduction, Classical and Contemporary Sources*, Santa Monica, Goodyear.

Bahro, R. (1986) *Building the Green Movement*, London, GMP.

— (1984) *From Red to Green*, London, Verso.

— (1982) *Socialism and Survival*, London, Heretic Books.

— (1978) *The Alternative in Eastern Europe*, London, New Left Books.

Beecher, J. and Bienvenu, R. (1975) *The Utopian Vision of Charles Fourier*, London, Jonathan Cape.

Bernstein, E. (1980) *Cromwell and Communism*, Nottingham, Spokesman.

— (1961) *Evolutionary Socialism*, New York, Schocken.

Bloch, E. (1975) 'A jubilee for renegades', *New German Critique*, 4, 18–25.

— (1972) *Atheism in Christianity*, New York, Herder & Herder.

— (1977) 'Nonsynchronism and the obligation to its dialectics', *New German Critique*, 11, 22–38.

— (1971) *On Karl Marx*, New York, Herder & Herder.

— (1986) *The Principle of Hope*, Oxford, Basil Blackwell.

Briggs, A, (1984) *William Morris: News from Nowhere and Selected Writings and Designs*, Harmondsworth, Penguin.

Caute, D. (1977) *The Fellow Travellers*, London, Quartet.

Connolly, J. (1971) *Labour in Irish History*, Dublin, New Books Publications.

Dunayevskaya, R. (1982) *Rosa Luxemburg, Women's Liberation, and Marx's Philosophy of Revolution*, Brighton, Harvester.

Edwards, O. D., and Ransom, B. (1973) *James Connolly: Selected Political Writings*, London, Jonathan Cape.

Ellis, P. B. (ed.) (1973) *James Connolly: Selected Writings*, Harmondsworth, Penguin.

Engels, F. (1975) *Anti-Dühring*, London, Lawrence & Wishart.

— (1975) *Socialism: Utopian and Scientific*, Peking, Foreign Languages Press.

Engels, F., Lafargue, P. and L. (1959) *Correspondence: Volume 1 1868–1886*, Moscow: Foreign Languages Publishing House.

155

Geoghegan, V. (1987) 'Marxism and utopianism', in Beauchamp, G., Roemer, K. and Smith, N. (eds) *Utopian Studies I*, Lanham, University Press of America.

— (1981) *Reason and Eros: The Social Theory of Herbert Marcuse*, London, Pluto.

Goode, P. (ed.) (1983) *Karl Kautsky: Selected Political Writings*, London, Macmillan.

Goodwin, B. and Taylor, K. (1982) *The Politics of Utopia*, London, Hutchinson.

Gorz, A. (1983) *Ecology as Politics*, London, Pluto.

— (1982) *Farewell to the Working Class: An Essay on Post-Industrial Socialism*, London, Pluto.

— (1985) *Paths to Paradise: On the Liberation from Work*, London, Pluto.

— (1975) *Socialism and Revolution*, London, Allen Lane.

Greaves, C. D. (1976) *The Life and Times of James Connolly*, London, Lawrence & Wishart.

Gurvitch, G. (1948) 'La sociologie du jeune Marx', *Cahiers Internationaux De Sociologie*, III, 3–47.

Haraszti, M. (1977) *A Worker in a Worker's State*, Harmondsworth, Penguin.

Harding, N. and Taylor, R. (1983) *Marxism in Russia: Key Documents 1879–1906*, Cambridge, Cambridge University Press.

Harrison, J. F. C. (1969) *Robert Owen and the Owenites in Britain and America: The Quest for the New Moral World*, London, Routledge & Kegan Paul.

Hegedus, A., Heller, A., Markus, M., and Vajda, M. (1976) *The Humanisation of Socialism: Writings of the Budapest School*, London: Allison & Busby.

Heller, A. (1976) *The Theory of Need in Marx*, London, Allison & Busby.

Hirsch, A. (1981) *The French New Left: An Intellectual History from Sartre to Gorz*, Boston, South End Press.

History of the Communist Party of the Soviet Union, (Bolsheviks) (1939), Moscow, Foreign Languages Publishing House.

Horsburgh, H. J. N. (1956) 'The relevance of the utopian', *Ethics*, LXVII, October 1956, 127–38.

Howard, D. (ed.) (1971) *Selected Political Writings of Rosa Luxemburg*, New York, Monthly Review Press.

Hudson, W. (1982) *The Marxist Philosophy of Ernst Bloch*, London, Macmillan.

Hunt, K. (1986) 'Crossing the river of fire: the socialist construction of women's politicization', in Evans, J. *et al. Feminism and Political Theory*, London, Sage.

Ionescu, G. (ed.) (1976) *The Political Thought of Saint-Simon*, Oxford, Oxford University Press.

Jameson, F. (1976) 'Introduction/Prospectus: to reconsider the relationship of Marxism to utopian thought', *The Minnesota Review*, N.S.VI, 53–8.

Jennings, J. R. (1985) *Georges Sorel: The Character and Development of His Thought*, Basingstoke, Macmillan/St Anthony's.

Katz, B. (1982) *Herbert Marcuse and the Art of Liberation*, London, Verso.

Kautsky, K. (1916) *The Social Revolution*, Chicago, Kerr & Co.

— (1979) *Thomas More and His Utopia*, London, Lawrence & Wishart.

Kellner, D. (1984) *Herbert Marcuse and the Crisis of Marxism*, Basingstoke, Macmillan.

Kenyon, T. (1982) 'Utopia in reality: "ideal" societies in social and political theory', *History of Political Thought*, III (1), January 1982, 123–55.

Knoll, S. B. (1984) 'Socialism as dystopia: political uses of utopian dime novels in pre World War I Germany', in Wilson, E. D. (ed.) *Society For Utopian Studies: Eighth Annual Conference*, Indiana, PA, Society for Utopian Studies.

Kolakowski, L. (1983) 'The death of utopia reconsidered', in McCurrin, S. (ed.) *The Tanner Lectures on Human Values IV*, Cambridge, Cambridge University Press, 229–47.

Kumar, K. (1987) *Utopia and Anti-Utopia in Modern Times*, Oxford, Basil Blackwell.

Lafargue, P. (1890) *The Evolution of Property from Savagery to Civilization*, London, Swan Sonnenschein.

— (n.d.) *The Right To Be Lazy*, Chicago, Charles H. Kerr.

Landmann, M. (1975) 'Talking with Ernst Bloch: Korcula, 1968', *Telos*, 25, 165–85.

Lasky, M. J. (1976) *Utopia and Revolution*, Chicago, Chicago University Press.

Lenin, V. I. (1960–80) *Collected Works*, London, Lawrence and Wishart.

Levitas, R. (1985) 'New right utopias', *Radical Philosophy*, 39, Spring 1985, 2–9.

Lukes, S. (1984) 'Marxism and utopianism', in Alexander, P. and Gill, R. *Utopias*, London, Duckworth, 153–67.

Luxemburg, R. (1979) *Comrade and Lover*, London, Pluto.

McLellan, D. (1976) *Marx's Grundrisse*, London, Granada.

Mannheim, K. (1936) *Ideology and Utopia*, London, Routledge & Kegan Paul.

Manuel, F. E. (1971) *Design for Utopia*, New York, Schocken.

— (1963) *The New World of Henri Saint-Simon*, Notre Dame, University of Notre Dame.

Manuel, F. E. and Manuel, F. P. (1979) *Utopian Thought in the Western World*, Oxford, Basil Blackwell.

Marcuse, H. (1972) *An Essay on Liberation*, Harmondsworth, Penguin.

— (1972) *Counter-Revolution and Revolt*, London, Allen Lane.

— (1972) *Eros and Civilisation*, London, Sphere.

— (1970) *Five Lectures*, London, Allen Lane.

— (1972) *Negations*, Harmondsworth, Penguin.

— (1972) *One Dimensional Man*, London, Sphere.

— (1968) *Reason and Revolution*, London, Routledge & Kegan Paul.

Marx, K. (1974) *The First International and After*, Harmondsworth, Penguin.

Marx, K. and Engels, F. (1975–) *Collected Works*, London, Lawrence & Wishart.

— (1958) *On Religion*, London, Lawrence & Wishart.

— (1980) *On the Paris Commune*, Moscow, Progress.

— (1975) *Selected Correspondence*, Moscow, Progress.

— (1970) *Selected Works*, London, Lawrence & Wishart.

— (1967) *The Communist Manifesto*, Harmondsworth, Penguin.

Meier, P. (1978) *William Morris: The Marxist Dreamer*, Hassocks, The Harvester Press.

Meisner, M. (1982) *Marxism Maoism and Utopianism*, Madison, The University of Wisconsin Press.

Miliband, R. (1979) 'A commentary on Rudolf Bahro's alternative', *The Socialist Register 1979*, London, Merlin.

Morris, M. (1936) *William Morris: Artist Writer Socialist*, Oxford, Basil Blackwell.

Morris, W. (1890) 'The development of modern society', *The Commonweal*, July–August, 1890.

Morton, A. L. (ed.) (1973) *Political Writings of William Morris*, London, Lawrence & Wishart.

— (ed.) (1968) *The Life and Ideas of Robert Owen*, London: Lawrence and Wishart.

— (ed.) (1973) *Three Works by William Morris*, London, Lawrence & Wishart.

Ollman, B. (1977) 'Marx's vision of communism: a reconstruction', *Critique*, 8, Summer 1977, 7–41.

Owen, R. (1967) *The Life of Robert Owen*, I, London, Frank Cass.

Plekhanov, G. (1977) *Selected Philosophical Works*, Moscow, Progress.

Portis, L. (1980) *Georges Sorel*, London, Pluto.

Poster, M. (1975) *Existential Marxism in Postwar France: From Sartre to Althusser*, Princeton, Princeton University Press.

— (1971) *Harmonian Man*, New York, Doubleday.

Ransom, B. (1980) *Connolly's Marxism*, London, Pluto.

Rohrlich, R. and Baruch, E. H. (1984) *Women in Search of Utopia: Mavericks and Mythmakers*, New York, Schocken.

Rowbotham, S. (1984) 'Hopes, dreams & dirty nappies', *Marxism Today*, December 1984, 8–12.

Rowbotham, S., Segal, L. and Wainwright, H. (1979) *Beyond The Fragments*, London, Merlin.

Salvadori, M. (1979) *Karl Kautsky and the Socialist Revolution 1880–1938*, London, New Left Books.

Singer, J. L. (1981) *Daydreaming and Fantasy*, Oxford, Oxford University Press.

Solomon, M. (1972) 'Marx and Bloch: reflection on utopia and art', *Telos*, 13, 68–85.

— (ed.) (1979) *Marxism and Art*, Hassocks, Harvester.

Spencer, M. C. (1981) *Charles Fourier*, Boston, Twayne.

Stanley, J. L. (ed.) (1976) *From Georges Sorel: Essays in Socialism and Philosophy*, New York, Oxford University Press.

Suvin, D. (1976) ' "Utopian" and "Scientific": two attributes for socialism from Engels', *The Minnesota Review*, N.S.VI, 59–70.

Taylor, K. (1975) (trans. and ed.), *Henri Saint-Simon: Selected writings on Science, Industry and Social Organisation*, London Croom Helm.
— (1982) *The Political Ideas of the Utopian Socialists*, London, Frank Cass.
Thompson, E. P. (1977) *William Morris: Romantic to Revolutionary*, London, Merlin.
Vajda, M. (1981) *The State and Socialism*, London, Allison & Busby.
Williams, R. (1980) 'Beyond actually existing socialism', *New Left Review*, 120, March/April 1980, 3–19.
Wolter, U. (ed.) (1980) *Rudolf Bahro: Critical Responses*, White Plains, M. E. Sharpe.
Wood, N. (1959) *Communism and British Intellectuals*, London, Gollancz.

INDEX